Let's Take It Outs

Edited by Kathy Charner, Mary Rein, and Brittany Roberts

Let's Take It OUTSIDE!

Teacher-Created Activities for Outdoor Learning

Edited by Kathy Charner, Mary Rein, and Brittany Roberts

Copyright ©2012 Gryphon House
Published by Gryphon House, Inc.
P.O. Box 10, Lewisville, NC 27023
800.638.0928; 877.638.7576 (fax)

Visit us on the web at www.gryphonhouse.com.

Cover photograph courtesy of iStock LP.

Library of Congress Cataloging-in-Publication Data

Let's take it outside! : teacher-created activities for outdoor learning / edited by Kathy Charner, Mary Rein, and Brittany Roberts
   p. cm.
 Summary: "Let's Take It Outside! combines the magic and excitement of the outdoors with activities that build math, literacy, and science skills in young children. Over 100 teacher-created, classroom-tested activities engage children's minds and bodies as they explore the limitless bounds of the outdoors!"-- Provided by publisher.
 ISBN 978-0-87659-395-0 (pbk.)
1. Outdoor education. 2. Outdoor education--Activity programs. I. Charner, Kathy. II. Rein, Mary B..
III. Roberts, Brittany.
 LB1047.L476 2012
 371.3'84--dc23
         2012011577

Bulk Purchase

Gryphon House books are available for special premiums and sales promotions as well as for fund-raising use. Special editions or book excerpts also can be created to specifications. For details, contact the Director of Marketing at Gryphon House.

Disclaimer

Gryphon House, Inc. cannot be held responsible for damage, mishap, or injury incurred during the use of or because of activities in this book. Appropriate and reasonable caution and adult supervision of children involved in activities, and corresponding to the age and capability of each child involved, is recommended at all times. Do not leave children unattended at any time. Observe safety and caution at all times.

Table of Contents

Introduction

Think back to your childhood and how you spent your free time. Most of us remember spending a great deal of that time outdoors. Perhaps neighborhood children would gather, and a spontaneous game of Kick the Can or Freeze Tag would ensue. Or perhaps an imagined town, such as the one in the story *Roxaboxen* by Alice McLerran, would be created out of twigs and stones lined up in patterns. Some of us recall making mud pies and creating mud cakes with berries picked from the bushes. And if there was a local playground, we challenged our physical skills with experiments on the monkey bars or swings. If our skills were not yet perfected and we fell in our attempts, we picked ourselves up, brushed ourselves off, and often tried again.

This is the excitement of outdoor play.

Today, children in child-care programs frequently have a very different outdoor experience. By necessity, it is often limited to shorter, defined periods of time that are also more limited in scope. Children are cautioned to stay out of the mud and told to use the equipment in a manner deemed safe by adults. This may interfere with a child's desire to take a risk or test a new, physically challenging skill. It is absolutely true that close supervision by adults who know the abilities of each and every child is crucial when it comes to outdoor play. However, while safety must always be at the forefront, children must also be provided with opportunities to learn and challenge themselves in ways that can only be achieved outdoors.

We do not always realize the complexity of children's outdoor learning. In the introduction to the CD, *Outdoor Play*, George Forman observes:

"When children play outdoors, we expect them to run, jump, and stretch beyond what is possible in the classroom. For this reason we often treat outdoor play as a time for large motor play, group games, and sports. Teachers less often consider the high-level thinking that occurs outdoors as children solve problems, negotiate rules, construct with loose parts, and figure out how to navigate changes in the terrain."

It is important to take a look at how outdoor play time is structured. Outdoor time is a prime opportunity for children to engage in self-selected, unstructured play. However, this does not imply that the adults should stand by or that they should avoid introducing engaging new activities to involve the children. Research has shown that adult presence and involvement can enhance learning for children. So, join in, be flexible, and enjoy the spontaneity and stimulation that outdoor play offers!

It's 10:30. The children are on the playground with their teachers. Two children carefully practice their balancing skills as they place one foot in front of another and walk across a 2-inch beam that the teacher has placed on the grass. A few children are taking turns going down the slide for the umpteenth time. Two other children are pretending that they are cooking as they fill a bucket with dirt and mix it with a stick. Another child is drawing with chalk on the sidewalk path. One other child is waiting to take his turn riding a tricycle.

In addition to unstructured play time, it is valuable for children to have outdoor activities that are focused on specific learning. The learning environments we create for children outdoors can be just as exciting as our indoor environments. Activity areas can be developed to provide children with opportunities for dramatic play, large motor movements, quiet activities, nature and science experiences, and art. The teacher-created activities in this book provide a wide range of possibilities to engage children's minds and bodies in invigorating and imaginative ways.

When we adjust our thinking to take advantage of everything the outdoors has to offer in the way of freshness, variety, and stimulation, even the simplest activity can take on a new meaning when we say, "*Let's Take It Outside!*"

On June 29, 2011 parents, teachers, children, and one elephant joined in the fun of International Mud Day . What began as an exchange between the children of Nepal and Australia, organized by Bishnu Bhatta and Gillian McAuliffe, is now an idea shared throughout the world.

~~~~

It is Thursday, and the forecast is for another day of rain and scattered showers. There is a muddy path full of puddles leading to the playground, and the worms have come out of hiding. The children have been cooped up inside. Why not go outside and play?

~~~~

Sources

"Outdoor Play," part of *The Learning Moments* series, produced by Videatives, Inc. and available at www.videatives.com
World Forum Foundation. http://worldforumfoundation.org/wf/wp/initiatives/nature-action-collaborative-for-children/international-mud-day-2011/stories

Michelle Barnea, Millburn, NJ

Chapter 1: Counting

There are many ways to incorporate counting and numbers into outdoor play. In this chapter you will find active games along with simple counting and sorting activities using natural objects. Let these ideas inspire your own creativity as you watch the children in their outdoor play.

Count the Action!

Learning Objective: To practice recognizing numerals, counting, listening, and following directions

Materials

2 bags, paper or fabric, large enough to hold the index cards
index cards
marker

Children's Books
1–2-3: A Child's First Counting Book by Alison Jay
My Little Counting Book by Roger Priddy
Pizza Counting by Christina Dobson

Preparation

- Make action picture cards. Use a simple stick figure to illustrate these actions: jumping, flapping arms, crouching, leaning to the left, leaning to the right, leaning forward with hands on hips, turning around, touching toes, and clapping.
- Make numeral cards showing the numerals 1–10 or select the range of numerals that are familiar to the children.
- Put the action picture cards into one bag and the numeral cards into the other.

What to Do

1. Divide the children into two teams. Choose one child from each team to begin.
2. One of these two children draws a numeral card and an action card from the bags.
3. All the children name the action and read the numeral card out loud.
4. The child from the other team performs the action as the entire group counts for him. For example, if the cards drawn were "touching toes" and "5," the child would touch his toes five times as the others count his actions.
5. Next, pick two new children, switch teams, and have the child from the opposite team draw the cards while the child from the first team performs the action. Continue until every child has had a turn.
6. For an extra challenge, count backward!

Susan Oldham Hill, Lakeland, FL

Leaf Scavenger Hunt

Learning Objectives: To review or learn colors; to practice counting objects; to practice number recognition; and to practice color recognition

Children's Books
Mouse's First Fall by
   Lauren Thompson
We're Going on a Leaf Hunt by
   Steve Metzger

Materials
markers
paper lunch bags

Preparation
- Check the playground and school grounds, and note the variety of colors of leaves available. If you live in an area where the leaves do not change much in the fall, you could make your own leaves out of colored paper and place them around the playground for the children to find.
- On each lunch bag, write a list of the colors and number of leaves for which that child is to hunt. For example, 4 red leaves, 3 brown leaves, and 2 orange leaves.

Tip: Use the matching color marker to write each color word.

What to Do
1. Read one of the suggested books about leaves and how they change color in the fall.
2. Pass out the bags to the children, one per child. Talk about how many leaves of each color they will need to collect.
3. Take a walk outside, and ask the children to collect and count their leaves and place them into their bags.
4. Sit with the children, and let them take turns counting the leaves of each color that they have discovered.
5. Ask the children to sort their leaves into big piles by color.

Darlene Taig, Westland, MI

Musical Number Hoops

Learning Objective: To count and to identify numerals

Materials
large plastic hoops
markers
music
number cards

Preparation
- Place six hoops in a large outdoor space.
- Write numbers and the corresponding number of dots on six cards. Make sure that the total adds up to the total number of children. For example, if you have 18 children you could have the following numbers on the six cards: 3, 6, 1, 2, 2, and 4.
- Place one card inside each hoop.

What to Do
1. Turn on music and have the children circle around, from hoop to hoop, as though they were playing musical chairs.
2. When the music stops, have the children gather inside the hoops in groups that match the numbers written on the cards inside. (If whole bodies do not fit inside the hoops, just have each child put one foot inside the hoop.)
3. Change the numbers each time you stop the music, so the children always have to look at the number inside the hoop and figure out if there is room for them inside.

Audrey Kanoff, Allentown, PA

Scoop, Pour, and Measure

Learning Objective: To become acquainted with typical units of measurement and to learn about their relationship to each other

Materials

clean plastic food containers in cup, pint, quart, and gallon sizes
masking tape
permanent marker
plastic measuring cups
sandbox
tote bag or crate

Preparation

- Using masking tape and a marker, label each container and measuring cup according to its size: *cup, pint, quart,* and *gallon.*
- Place the measuring cups and containers into a tote bag or crate.

What to Do

1. Take the children outside to the sandbox. Show them the measuring cups and food containers.
2. Ask a volunteer to fill a measuring cup with sand, then ask him to pour the sand into one of the containers (for instance, the gallon container). Ask the children to guess how many cups of sand it will take to fill the container.
3. As the volunteer fills the container, help the children count as each cup of sand is poured.
4. When the container is full, ask the children to recall how many cups of sand were measured (1 pint = 2 cups; 1 quart = 4 cups; 1 gallon = 16 cups).
5. Continue the process with each container.
6. Allow the children to continue measuring on their own. Encourage them to see how many pints will fill the quart container (two), how many quarts will fill the gallon container (four), and how many pints will fill the gallon container (eight).

Tip: Extend this activity by using water to measure and pour.

Rob Sanders, Brandon, FL

Sidewalk Number Line

Learning Objective: To learn to recognize numerals on a number line

Materials

chalk
sidewalk or other paved area

Children's Books

Number Lines: How Far to the Car
    by John Burstein
Rock It, Sock It, Number Line by
    Bill Martin Jr.

What to Do

1. As the children watch, write the numerals from 1 to 10 on the sidewalk. Put one numeral in each sidewalk square. If the squares aren't uniform, divide the sidewalk evenly with a chalk line. (If no pavement is available, use cones or chairs with signs.)
2. Demonstrate moving on the number line. Stand on the numeral 4, for example, then move two forward and end up on the numeral 6.
3. Ask a child to stand on that numeral. Then ask him, "Where are you?" The child and the other children will answer, "Six!"
4. Give various directions, such as, "Take four steps backward."
5. All the children count with the child on the number line as he walks or jumps four steps backward. Ask him, "Where are you?" The child and the other children will answer, "Two!"
6. Give the child another direction such as, "Take three steps forward. Where are you?" Continue with another child.
7. Sing this song to the tune of "Do You Know the Muffin Man?"
    Oh, I am on the number line, the number line, the number line.
    Oh, I am on the number line, moving up and down.
    I like to count on the number line, the number line, the number line.
    One, two, three, four, five, six, seven, eight, nine, ten.

Susan Oldham Hill, Lakeland, FL

Water Bag Toss

Learning Objective: To practice recognizing numerals from 1 to 9

Materials

9 Hula-Hoops
18 zipper-seal plastic bags
set of numeral cards, 1–9
tape
water

Children's Books

1–2–3: A Child's First Counting Book by Alison Jay
Counting Crocodiles by Judy Sierra
The Icky Bug Counting Book by Jerry Pallotta

Preparation

- Fill the plastic bags with water and seal them. Make extra bags in case of breakage.
- Arrange the Hula-Hoops into three groups of three hoops each.
- Tape the numeral cards to the outside edges of the hoops, one card on each hoop. Start with 1, 2, and 3 on the first set of hoops. Tape 4, 5, and 6 on the next set; and tape 7, 8, and 9 on the third set of hoops.

Tip: The numeral cards will get wet and dirty. If possible, laminate the cards or place them in zipper-seal bags before the activity begins.

What to Do

1. Divide the children into three groups. Line up each group a few feet from one of the sets of three hoops.
2. The children toss water bags into the hoops. Give the first child in each line an appropriate number of water bags for the set of hoops in front of him. Ask the child to toss into the hoop the number of bags that matches the numeral taped onto one of the hoops. For example, for the hoop with the numeral 2 on it, a child would toss in two water bags. For the hoop with the numeral 8 on it, the child would toss in eight water bags.
3. Continue until every child in each group has had a turn to toss in water bags.
4. Rotate the groups of children to the next set of hoops, and continue until every child has counted all of the numerals 1–9.

Susan Oldham Hill, Lakeland, FL

Wonderful Web

Learning Objective: To recognize numerals

Children's Book
The Very Busy Spider by Eric Carle

Materials

large ball of yarn, any color
number cards (index cards with the numbers 1–10 written in
   black pen)
tape

Preparation

• Write one number and the corresponding number of dots onto each index card. Shuffle the cards.

What to Do

1. Look for spiderwebs outside. When you find one, talk with the children about the strands in the web.
2. Ask the children to sit in a circle. Tell them that they are going to make their own spiderweb.
3. Shuffle the cards and give one to each child. Help the children identify the number on their card by recognizing the numeral or counting the dots.
4. Give the child with number *one* the end of the yarn and collect his card.
5. Unwind the ball of yarn until you reach the child with the number *two*. Collect his card and ask him to hold onto the yarn.
6. Continue counting, unwinding yarn, and collecting cards until everyone is holding onto the yarn and you have collected all the cards.
7. Now ask everyone to continue to hold onto the yarn and stand up. Examine the spiderweb you have created!
8. Carefully place the web onto the ground. Ask the children how their web is the same or different from a spider's web.
9. Roll up the yarn, shuffle the number cards, and make a new web!

Norma Jorgensen, St. Paul, MN

Chapter 2: Alphabet

Connect alphabet learning with hands-on experiences in the outdoors to engage children's excitement about literacy. Offer these games and activities, and watch children's interest blossom.

Alphabet Nature Hunt

Learning Objective: To connect letter sounds with beginning sounds in words

Materials
crayons and markers, optional
paper (optional)
pen or pencil
spiral notebook

Preparation
* Write each letter of the alphabet on a separate page in the notebook.

What to Do
1. Ask the children to look and listen for things in nature. Explain that you are going to make an ABC book of what they find.
2. Guide the children to sit on the ground with you. Ask each child what she sees or hears—for example, a bird, grass, or dirt.
3. When a child responds, guide the group to repeat the word, paying attention to the beginning sound: "Sharon sees a bird. **B**-ird."
4. Encourage a volunteer to identify the beginning letter. Make corrections as needed. Write the word in the notebook on the appropriate letter page, and show the word to the children.
5. Continue until each child has had a turn. If you run out of items to identify, walk to another location, and repeat the process. If the children have difficulty choosing different items to identify, use an *I Spy* approach to help them identify additional items. For instance: "I spy something white and fluffy in the sky."
6. After the hunt, review the nature words. Turn the pages of the ABC book and read the words for each letter.
7. Extend this activity by encouraging the children to use markers or crayons and illustrate each word.

Tip: Keep this book in your classroom library, and add to it when the children discover new nature words. If you are unable to find things in your environment for certain letters, encourage the children to look through magazines and books for natural objects, plants, and animals to fill in the missing letters.

Rob Sanders, Brandon, FL

Fun with Swirly Letters

Learning Objective: To recognize letters and shapes

Children's Book
Harold and the Purple Crayon by Crockett Johnson

Materials
bowl of water for rinsing hands
shaving cream
table with a smooth surface, or several trays

What to Do
This is an activity that is often done indoors, but it is a natural for "Let's Take It Outside!" on a warm day.
1. Squirt some shaving cream onto the tabletop or the trays.
2. Model drawing letters and shapes in the shaving cream with your finger.
3. Depending on the ages of the children, either let them play freely in the slippery soap, or ask them to imitate the letters and shapes you draw.
4. Replenish the shaving cream as needed.

Monica Hay Cook, Tucson, AZ

Mud Dough Letters

Learning Objectives: To form three-dimensional letters and identify them by sight; to use uppercase and lowercase letters (when children are ready); to follow directions

Materials
bucket or tub
dry sand or gravel for sprinkling
flat piece of wood, cardboard, or a big baking sheet
mud dough (see recipe)
natural materials, such as pinecones, crushed dry leaves, small twigs, and so on
plastic cups and containers
play clothes
scrub brush
soap
towels
water

Children's Books
How to Make a Mudpie by Rozanne Lanczak Williams
Mud! by Wendy Cheyette Lewison
Mud Book by John Cage and Lois Long

Mud Dough Recipe
2 cups mud
2 cups sand
½ cup salt
enough water to make the dough pliable

Preparation
- The children should wear comfortable, washable play clothes.
- Have a hose or bucket of fresh water handy for rinsing hands and an old towel for drying. Thorough washing can take place at a sink with soap and warm water at the end of the activity.

What to Do
1. Choose a place to create, such as the sidewalk or grass.
2. Let the children help mix the mud dough by hand. The dough should be pliable.
3. Encourage the children to explore the dough in any way, eventually rolling "snakes."
4. Ask them to make any letters they know with the snakes, perhaps letters from their own names.
5. Make a letter, and ask the children what letter it is. They can imitate making the same letter.

6. Look around—if you made an *S*, do you see the sun or a stick? Talk about letters and words. Continue, enjoying making letters and talking about their sounds and shapes.
7. When nearing completion, encourage each child to make a mud dough letter that can be decorated with sand, gravel, crushed leaves, and other outdoor collage finds.
8. Place the letters on a baking sheet or a piece of cardboard or wood to dry. You may wish to etch each child's name onto the bottom or side of her letter with a toothpick.
9. When done, use a hose, bucket, scrub brush, or whatever is necessary to clean the mud dough area, especially if it was on a sidewalk or playground area. Grass may just be rinsed.
10. Dry the letters overnight.

Related Fingerplays, Songs, and Poems

"Sing a Song for Mud Pies"
© 2011 MaryAnn F. Kohl
(To the tune of "Sing a Song of Sixpence")
Sing a song for mud pies,
You don't need a plan.
Mix it 'til it's mooshy,
Pat it with your hand.
Put it on a pan and
Leave it in the sun.
Wait and wait and wait a while.
Now, I think it's done!

"Mud, Mud, I Love Mud"
© 2011 MaryAnn F. Kohl
(To the tune of "Row, Row, Row Your Boat")
Mud, mud, I love mud,
See me squish and squeeze!
Stir and poke and stir and poke,
Make a mud pie, please.

Mud, mud, mud is fun
Hear it blop and bloop.
Between my fingers and my toes
Making muddy soup.

Mud, mud, I love mud,
See me squish and squeeze!
Stir and poke and stir and poke,
Make a mud pie, please.

MaryAnn F. Kohl, Bellingham, WA

Letter Grab Bag

Learning Objective: To learn letter shapes using the sense of touch; to recognize letters and their sounds

Materials
large alphabet letters
paper or cloth bag

Children's Books
ABC Safari by Karen Lee
K Is for Kitten by Niki Clark Leopold
A Very Active Alphabet: And Other Alphabet Rhymes illustrated by Kate Somme

What to Do

1. Before going on a walk outdoors, talk with the children about what you are likely to see, and select three letters to put into the bag. For example, an *L* for leaf, a *B* for bird, an *S* for sidewalk.
2. Talk about these letters—their sounds and shapes.
3. Put the letters into the bag and head outside for your walk.
   Tip: If your group is young or inexperienced, put only two letters into the bag.
4. When a child says, "I see a bird!" let her reach into the bag and try to identify the letter *B* by touch.
5. Encourage each member of your group to notice something on the walk and to identify the appropriate letter by touch only. Talk about the shapes and what clues you can use as you search with your fingers.

Donna Alice Patton, Hillsboro, OH

Toss-and-Tell Letters Game

Learning Objective: To practice large motor skills and letter identification

Materials

3 beanbags
5 buckets
5 letter cards (choose the letters you want to focus on this week)
sidewalk chalk
tape

Preparation

- Tape a letter card to the side of each of the five buckets.
- Set up the buckets on a sidewalk or blacktop area.
- Draw a chalk line for the children to stand on.

What to Do

1. The children can take turns standing on the chalk line and throwing a beanbag into a bucket. Let each turn last until the child succeeds, but after the third miss, have the child move closer to the bucket for her next throw.
2. When the beanbag lands in a bucket, ask the child to name the letter on the bucket.
3. Repeat until each child has had a turn. Continue as long as the children are interested.

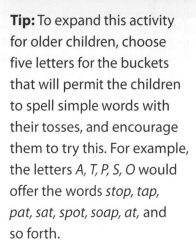

Tip: To expand this activity for older children, choose five letters for the buckets that will permit the children to spell simple words with their tosses, and encourage them to try this. For example, the letters *A, T, P, S, O* would offer the words *stop, tap, pat, sat, spot, soap, at,* and so forth.

Tracey Neumarke, Chicago, IL

Twiggy ABCs

Learning Objective: To experience letters with the sense of touch

Materials

collection of thin, dry twigs the children have gathered outdoors, and other small natural materials

markers

poster board or lightweight cardboard cut into 8" or 9" squares

white glue in squeeze bottles

Preparation

* Decide if there are particular letters you want to feature in this activity, and write them with markers on poster board squares.

What to Do

Set up this activity at a table outdoors so the children can add to the materials as needed.

1. Take the materials outside.
2. Model how to form letters with the twigs and other materials. Show how you can break some of the twigs to get the shapes you need.
3. Encourage the children to try it. Some may want to copy your letters, some may want to write a letter on a piece of poster board and lay their twigs on top of the lines, and some may want to make their letters free-form.
4. When they seem to be ready, show them how to draw a letter with glue on the poster board and lay twigs on the glue to form a permanent "twiggy letter."

Children's Books

Biscuit's ABC's by
    Alyssa Satin Capucilli
S Is for Snowman by
    Kathy-jo Wargin
Sounds and Letters by
    Ruth Owen

Donna Alice Patton, Hillsboro, OH

Bottle Bowling

Learning Objectives: To recognize letters; to practice large motor skills by rolling a ball toward a target

Materials

9-inch playground ball
craft paper, cut into six 5" x 15" strips
glue or tape
markers
sidewalk chalk
six 2-liter soda bottles with caps
water

Tip: Ball retrieval will be easier if you are able to set up your alley with a wall or other barrier directly behind the pins. You can probably get some enthusiastic volunteers from among the children to help with ball retrieval and pin setup.

Preparation

- Write a different letter onto each paper strip. Use letters the children are learning, and write the letters large enough to be seen easily from a distance.
- Wrap each paper around the middle of a bottle and attach it with glue or tape.
- Fill each bottle with about 3 inches of water. Cap tightly.
- Draw a bowling lane with chalk on the pavement, approximately 3 feet wide and 8 feet long.
- Set up the bottles (pins) at one end. Arrange the pins in a triangle shape with one bottle in front, two bottles behind it, and three bottles in the back row.

What to Do

1. Show the children how to roll the ball toward the target with one hand to the side or with both hands between their legs.
2. When a child knocks over one of the bottles, ask her to name the letter written on it.
3. Allow each child to keep rolling the ball until she knocks over one or more pins before moving on to the next player.
4. Reset the pins and proceed until all children have had a sufficient number of turns.

**Susan Arentson Sharkey,
Fletcher Hills, CA**

Letters, Letters Everywhere

Learning Objective: To recognize letters everywhere—even in architecture and in nature

Materials

8" x 10" pieces of poster board, one per child
alphabet stickers (optional)
crayons
markers
ruler
sticky stars (optional)

Preparation

- Draw two columns on the poster boards, and draw 26 lines (one for each letter of the alphabet).

What to Do

1. Help the children write the alphabet along the left side of their poster boards (or use alphabet stickers instead).
2. As you walk around outside, model the process of finding letters everywhere—on signs, in architecture, or in nature. Does a tree have two branches that form a *Y*? What about the *T* formed by two buildings or the *S* on a street sign?
3. For each letter the children find, ask them to make an *X* or put a sticky star in the box opposite the letter on their poster boards.
4. When you have completed your search, discuss how many letters the children found and where they found them.

Children's Books

A Fabulous Fair Alphabet by Debra Frasier
LMNO Peas by Keith Baker
Peter Blake's ABC by Peter Blake

Donna Alice Patton, Hillsboro, OH

Chapter 3: Colors

Outdoors is a natural color "laboratory." Take advantage of the colors outside to teach children the names of colors and to cultivate children's color recognition and an aesthetic sense for subtle color differences. Encourage children to share the excitement of their discoveries more freely outdoors than the four walls of a classroom allow.

Bubble Color Prints

Learning Objectives: To recognize colors; to develop small motor skills; to practice following directions

Children's Book
Pop! A Book About Bubbles by Kimberly Brubaker Bradley

Materials

bubble solution
large bowls (one for each pair of children)
liquid tempera paint (variety of colors)
paper
plastic straws
scissors
smocks or T-shirts

Preparation

- Put an inch or two of bubble solution into the bowls. Leave plenty of empty space in each bowl.
- Add a few drops of paint to each, and stir to make a colored bubble solution.
- Cut a small hole in each of the straws to prevent the children from sucking in the bubble solution.

What to Do

1. Pair up the children. Give each pair a bowl of colored bubble solution. Talk about the different colors. Help the children name each color.
2. Give each child a straw, and let them practice blowing out. It will help them to focus if you ask them to take the straws out of their mouths after each blow, take a deep breath, and then put the straw back in and blow again.
3. Now, let the children blow into the bubble solution. What happens when they blow really hard? What happens when they blow gently? Can they make big bubbles? small bubbles?
4. When the children have sufficiently explored making lots of bubbles and have completely filled their bowls to the brim, hand out the paper.
5. Help the children lay the paper on top of the colored bubbles to make bubble prints.
6. Set the bubble prints aside to dry. Display them in the classroom.

Ann Scalley, Orleans, MA

Shaving Cream Colors

Learning Objectives: To recognize and mix colors; to form and name shapes and letters

Materials

bowl of water for hand rinsing
food coloring
measuring cup
shaving cream
zipper-seal plastic bags, one per child

What to Do

This is another activity that is often done indoors. If you "Take It Outside!" you can use larger plastic bags and allow for the possibility of messiness without worry.

1. Place ½ cup shaving cream in each plastic bag. (Add more for a larger bag.)
2. Ask each child to put one or two drops of food coloring into his bag. Does he want to experiment? Use two different colors!
3. Squeeze most of the air out of the bag and zip it closed.
4. Have the children mix the shaving cream and food coloring by kneading the bags.
5. Now the children can draw with their fingers on the plastic and watch the shapes appear and disappear in the colored soap.

**Charlene M. Roediger,
Allentown, PA**

Snow Colors

Learning Objectives: To identify colors; to develop large motor skills and creativity

Materials
empty spray bottles (one for each child)
food coloring
plastic sand buckets, sand molds and shovels
snowy day
warm clothing
water

What to Do
1. On a snowy day, give each child an empty spray bottle filled with water.
2. Ask each child to choose a color; add a few drops of that food coloring to the water.
3. Take the children outside with buckets, molds, shovels, and spray bottles.
4. Encourage the children to make snow castles and other sand-mold structures and then spray the structures with the colored water in the bottles.

Lisa Chichester, Parkersburg, WV

LET'S TAKE IT OUTSIDE

Stone Search

Learning Objective: To practice color matching

Materials
4 egg cartons
48 stones
paint and paintbrushes

Children's Books
If You Find a Rock by
    Peggy Christian
Rocks and Minerals by
    Chris Pellant
Stone Soup by Marcia Brown

What to Do
1. Divide stones into four groups of 12 and paint them four different colors. Paint the egg cartons corresponding colors.
2. Hide the stones on the playground and put the egg cartons in a central location.
3. When the children go outside to play, ask them to hunt for the stones and put each one into the appropriate egg carton.

Ellen Domenico, Ewing Twp., NJ

Color, May I?

Learning Objective: To recognize color names

Materials
none needed

What to Do
1. Explain to the children that in this outdoor game they will be thinking of something to match the color that will be named. It could be something they can see outside or something they know about but cannot see.
2. One child will be the leader. The others line up as in the traditional Mother, May I? game. The leader chooses a color, such as yellow. Each child in line must name something yellow, such as a banana, the sun, or a shirt someone is wearing that day. When an appropriate item is named, the child can take three giant steps toward the designated finish line.
3. Continue with several other colors until everyone reaches the finish line.
4. Choose another leader and repeat the game.

Children's Books
The Black Book of Colors by Menena Cottin
A Book About Color by Mark Gonyea
A Color of His Own by Leo Lionni
Counting Colors by Roger Priddy

Susan Oldham Hill, Lakeland, FL

Rainbow Scavenger Hunt

Learning Objectives: To practice identifying colors; to follow verbal instructions

Materials
markers in blue, green, orange, purple, red, and yellow
poster board

Preparation
• Use the markers to draw a rainbow on the poster board. Make each band of color wide enough to be easily seen.

What to Do
1. Read a book about rainbows to the children.
2. Show the children your drawing of a rainbow (or photographs of real rainbows). Ask them if they have ever seen a rainbow. Talk about how all the rainbow colors can be found in nature if we look carefully.
3. When you go outside to play, ask the children to search for something blue. Encourage them to look for natural objects that are blue rather than human-made items.
4. Repeat, helping the children locate something that is purple. If there is nothing purple in your area, discuss what they might find elsewhere: flowers, berries, grapes, or a butterfly. Can you find pictures of natural purple items in books or magazines? Could you find something purple if you were searching your area in a different season?
5. Repeat, helping the children locate each color in turn.

Children's Books
All the Colors of the Rainbow by Allen Fowler
Color Me a Rhyme by Jane Yolen
What Color Is Nature? by Stephen R. Swinburne

Tip: Be prepared to talk about the difference between natural items and human-made objects.

Sue Bradford Edwards, Florissant, MO

Sidewalk Color Sort

Learning Objective: To practice classifying by color

Materials
sidewalk chalk in primary colors
sidewalk

What to Do

1. Using chalk, write the names of colors on sidewalk sections as the children watch and "read along." Write *red* with the red chalk, and so on.
2. Move the children back from the sidewalk about 15 feet.
3. Ask the children to look at their shirts and to name the color they see. Help children wearing prints or stripes choose one color to name.
4. Now ask everyone to move to the square on the sidewalk that matches the chosen color from their shirts.
5. When the children are on the squares, talk about who is in each square and how they match the color on the sidewalk.
6. Repeat with the following color choices: color of their shoes, their shorts, their hair, their eyes, their favorite colors, their backpacks, and so on.

Children's Books
The Black Book of Colors by Menena Cottin
A Book About Color by Mark Gonyea
A Color of His Own by Leo Lionni

Tip: On some choices, such as color of hair and eyes, the sidewalk areas will be crowded. Remind the children to be careful not to run into a friend. Rewrite the color words on the sidewalk as necessary.

Susan Oldham Hill, Lakeland, FL

Sidewalk Colors

Learning Objective: To recognize color names

Materials
CD player (battery operated) and a CD of lively music
sidewalk chalk
sidewalk

Preparation
- Divide eight (or more) sidewalk squares in half to make two-way traffic. You need to have at least as many sidewalk halves as you have children in your group.
- Choose two or three colors of sidewalk chalk, and color a solid area of one color in each of the sidewalk halves, so the children can walk up one side and down the other, stepping on different colors as they go.

What to Do
1. Explain to the children that in this game, they will walk on the colors on the sidewalk. When they get to one end of a line of colors, they will turn and go back down the line on the other side.
2. The children will continue going around until the music stops. When it stops, they will take turns naming the color on which they stand. Start the music again and repeat several times to give the children more opportunities to name colors.

Children's Books
The Black Book of Colors by
    Menena Cottin
A Book About Color by
    Mark Gonyea
A Color of His Own by Leo Lionni
Counting Colors by Roger Priddy

Tip: For an added challenge, increase the number of colors on the sidewalk to four or five.

Susan Oldham Hill, Lakeland, FL

Leaves in the Wind

Learning Objective: To practice matching shapes and colors

Children's Books
Leaf Man by Lois Ehlert
Leaves by David Ezra Stein
Leaves by Vijaya Bodach

Materials

12" tag board leaf cutouts (5 of each shape: oak, maple, elm) colored red, brown, and yellow
3 more 12" tag board leaf cutouts (natural color): oak, maple, and elm

adult scissors
construction paper in red, brown, and yellow
glue
leaf stencils: oak, maple, and elm
markers

Preparation

- Trace leaf shapes onto tag board.
- Cut out five of each type and color them, or glue on construction paper in red, brown, and yellow.
- Cut one of each type of leaf from the tag board (so the children can focus on the shape of the leaf instead of the color).
- Set aside one sheet each of the red, brown, and yellow construction paper.

What to Do

1. Discuss the shapes of the leaves and name the trees from which they come. Show photographs of the leaves or actual leaves they can touch.
2. Set up six areas using any prominent features of your outdoor area.
3. Choose three children to hold up pieces of construction paper, and three others to hold the plain leaf shapes. Station each child in one of the six areas.
4. Distribute one colored leaf shape to each of the remaining children.
5. When you say, "Color!" the children with the colored leaves are to run to the child holding the paper that matches the color of the leaf they have. When you say, "Shape!" the children should run to the child whose leaf shape matches their own.
6. For added fun, call out, "Wind!" At this signal, the children should twirl and "blow" around the playground. If you are doing this activity on a windy day, there may be real leaves blowing in the wind for the children to imitate.

Susan Oldham Hill, Lakeland, FL

Chapter 4: Shapes

When children play outdoors, you can help them connect abstract shapes with the real world around them. Many people think of rectangles and squares in buildings, fences, signs, and pavement. But consider tall straight tree trunks, circular flowers with oval petals, smooth round rocks, and triangular bits of gravel. Our world is made up of shapes! The shape-recognition games and activities in this chapter will help children connect indoor shapes with those found outside.

3+

Block Stamps

Learning Objective: To develop small motor skills and shape recognition

Materials

blocks of all sizes and shapes
large paper
liquid tempera paint
trays or cookie sheets, one for every three children

What to Do

This is a simple activity that can be done indoors or out, but if you "Take It Outside!" it adds to the fun!

1. Cover an outdoor table or other surface with large sheets of paper.
2. Pour paint onto cookie sheets or trays. Two or three children may share a tray of paint and one sheet of paper.
3. Ask the children to choose a wooden block shape and stamp it into the paint and onto the paper.
4. Talk about what shapes the children are creating. Are there rectangles? squares?
5. As the children keep stamping, help them notice the shapes and patterns that appear.

Sarah Stonebraker, Seattle, WA

Make Your Own Blocks

3+

Learning Objectives: To practice shape recognition, small motor skills, and increased attention span

Materials

liquid tempera paint
paintbrushes
paper cups or other paint containers
sandpaper
wood scraps

Preparation

- Go to a home-improvement store or a construction site, and ask them for untreated wood scraps.

What to Do

Enjoy this project over a period of several days.

1. On a table outdoors, set out the wood scraps and the sandpaper. Show the children how to sand the rough edges of the wood. Let the children work at their own pace over several days. You may have to do the finishing touches.
2. When the wood is smooth enough to paint, put away the sandpaper, clean up the sawdust, and set out the painting supplies.
3. Ask the children to select pieces of wood to paint. Which shapes did they choose? Help the children identify the shapes.
4. Let the children paint the wooden shapes any color they choose.
5. Set the shapes somewhere they will not be disturbed, and let the paint dry.
6. When they are dry, use the shapes in your block area along with the blocks you have. The children will love to build with blocks that they made themselves!

Sarah Stonebraker, Seattle, WA

3+

Shape Songs

Learning Objective: To recognize shapes

Materials
chalk
large, paved space outdoors

What to Do
1. Ahead of time, use chalk to draw a large circle on the pavement, large enough for four or five children to stand inside.
2. Teach the children this simple song to the tune of "Someone's in the Kitchen with Dinah."
   Someone's in the circle with Jason,
   Someone's in the circle, it's true-oo-oo-oo.
   Someone's in the circle with Jason,
   Waiting for a friend like you!
3. Choose a child to stand inside the circle; the remaining hold hands in a circle around the child in the middle and sing the song together.
4. Ask the child inside the circle to choose a friend to join her. Continue until the circle is full, and then choose a new leader.
5. Repeat with a large square, triangle, and so on.
6. As a variation, collect items that are the same shape to place into the large chalked shape.

Susan Oldham Hill, Lakeland, FL

LET'S TAKE IT OUTSIDE

Hoppity Shapes

Learning Objectives: To identify common geometric shapes by name and by sight; to follow directions; to follow simple rules and to take turns

Materials
chalk
playground
sidewalk, driveway, or other paved area

Preparation
- Draw some large shapes with chalk, making them close together on the sidewalk or play area. Some common shapes to begin with are circle, square, triangle, and star.
- Write the name of the shape inside each shape.

What to Do
1. Ask several children, no more than five, to stand in front of a shape. Encourage the children to hop around to any other shape they wish.
2. After they have done this for a while, ask all of the children to hop to one particular shape. For example, say, "Hop to the square!" Do this for each shape you have drawn.
3. To increase the challenge, say, "Hop to any shape *except* the triangle." Or, "Hop to all the shapes but *not* the square."
4. Vary the game by saying, "If you are wearing something that is red, hop to the diamond. If you are wearing something that is yellow, hop to the oval."
5. Next say, "Everyone find a shape to rest on." Allow the children time to rest.

Children's Books
I Spy Shapes in Art by
   Lucy Micklethwait
Shapes, Shapes, Shapes by
   Tana Hoban

Tip: To play with a large group, simply draw more shapes. It's perfectly fine to have more than one circle or many squares. The fun and learning are the same.

MaryAnn F. Kohl, Bellingham, WA

I Spy Shape Hunt

Learning Objective: To recognize and name geometric shapes

Materials
poster board
ruler
scissors

Preparation
- Cut the following geometric shapes from poster board: 8" x 8" square, 8" x 14" rectangle, 8" diameter circle, and 8" x 8" x 8" triangle.

Tip: Don't be afraid of using mathematical vocabulary with young children. You are laying the groundwork for continued learning.

What to Do
1. Introduce the shapes to the children. Say the name of each shape, and ask the children to repeat the name.
2. Talk about the distinguishing characteristics of each shape. For example, a square has four equal sides and four corners; a rectangle has four sides, with opposite sides being parallel, and four corners; a circle has no straight edges or corners; a triangle has three sides and three corners.
3. Bring along your shapes, and take the children on an outdoor hunt for shapes. Locate a shape, such as the rectangular side of the building, and say, "I spy a rectangle."
4. Allow one of the children to hold the rectangular poster board shape as the other children look around for a rectangle. Encourage the children to make guesses about where the rectangle you spied is located. Compare the poster board shape with the shapes they identify.
5. If the children cannot find the shape, give additional hints, such as, "My rectangle is made of bricks," or "My rectangle has two rectangles in the middle of it."

Rob Sanders, Brandon, FL

Shape Match-Ups

Learning Objective: To practice shape recognition

Materials
hole punch
laminating machine (optional)
set of shape cards for each child (rectangle, circle, square, triangle)
yarn

Children's Books
Greedy Triangle by Marilyn Burns
Mouse Shapes by
    Ellen Stohl Walsh
Shapes, Shapes, Shapes by
    Tana Hoban

Preparation
* Make a set of sturdy tagboard shape cards for each child.
  Laminate them if possible. Tie each set together with yarn.

What to Do
This is a good activity to do with the children after helping them to recognize shapes with the I Spy Shape Hunt activity.

1. Discuss shapes with the children, noticing straight or curved sides and counting sides and corners.
2. Distribute the shape-card sets to each child.
3. Take a shape walk. As you notice a shape, for example a rectangular window, show it to the children, name it, and ask the children to hold up the matching shape card from their sets.
4. Focus the children's attention onto the shapes they see on the playground, on a building, in the parking lot, or around the block.
5. Take walks to different areas and ask the children to notice the shapes they see. Can they find all the shapes in each area, or is it easier to find certain shapes in certain places?

Susan Oldham Hill, Lakeland, FL

Shape Toss

Learning Objectives: To practice shape recognition; to practice large motor skills

Materials
construction paper
contact paper
laminating machine (optional)
markers
scissors
small cube-shaped box with a lid that can be fastened securely

Preparation
- Cut out six large shapes from construction paper.
- On the back of each shape, write movement instructions. For example: *Hop three times; Turn in a circle; Squat down and jump.*
- Laminate the shapes or cover them with clear contact paper.
- On each side of the box, use the markers to draw one of the shapes.

What to Do
You will appreciate having plenty of outdoor space for this activity.
1. Arrange the paper shapes into a circle, leaving space in the middle.
2. Have all the children stand around the circle.
3. Toss the shape box into the middle of the circle. Help the children name and describe the shape on the top of the box.
4. If necessary, help the children find the paper shape that the box is showing.
5. Once the children are comfortable finding the shapes, add the movement component. When the children find a given shape, talk about the movement words written on that shape. For example, the triangle might read, "Jump three times." The circle might read, "Spin around."
6. Do the movement all together!
7. Toss the box again and find a different shape. Do that movement together!

Sarah Stonebraker, Seattle, WA

LET'S TAKE IT OUTSIDE

Mapping the Great Outdoors

Learning Objectives: To explore the concept of mapping; to practice shape recognition

Materials

markers
poster board
sidewalk chalk in the same colors as the markers

Preparation

- Using the sidewalk chalk, draw a map on the playground or a driveway. You can include trees (green circles), mountains (purple triangles), fields (brown squares), and a lake (blue oval).
- Draw a legend on the poster board using the same colors and shapes.

Children's Books

Follow That Map! by Scot Ritchie
Mapping Penny's World by Loreen Leedy
Me on the Map by Joan Sweeney
Where Do I Live? by Neil Chesanow

Tip: If the children are eager to explore maps further, you could use sidewalk chalk to draw a map of your yard, the school grounds, or the surrounding neighborhood.

What to Do

1. Read one of the suggested books about maps with the children.
2. Discuss how maps picture the landscape. They can show streets and houses or mountains, lakes, and streams.
3. Ask the children what they see drawn on the pavement. What do they think the various shapes represent?
4. Now show the children the legend. Point to the green circles. Can they find the trees on the map? As a group or individually, have the children locate and stand on the various features.
5. Discuss what else they could include on a map.

**Sue Bradford Edwards,
Florissant, MO**

LET'S TAKE IT OUTSIDE

Chapter 5: Art

Think of your favorite artists. How many of them found inspiration outdoors? Children certainly can be inspired by the beauty of nature, but they can also respond to the freedom and wider vistas of an outdoor setting. In this chapter you will find art activities planned for the outdoors, and activities that use natural materials to make art. But as you expand your vision of outdoor play, think of art projects you usually do indoors that could be adapted, then say, "Let's take it outside!"

ART

A Brush with Nature

Learning Objectives: To encourage creativity; to develop small and large motor skills

Related Books
Elmer and the Rainbow by David McKee
I Ain't Gonna Paint No More! by Karen Beaumont

Materials

empty margarine tub with lid
large roll of paper or an old white sheet
liquid dish soap
natural materials, such as leaves, twigs, and stones
plastic plates or pie tins
powdered tempera paint, any color(s) but red
water

Preparation

- Mix the powdered paint with water and a little dish soap to make a thick paint that barely drips. Keep it in the covered margarine tub until needed.
- Be sure there is a source of water nearby, or fill a bucket with water for washing.
- Pour the paint mixture into the plastic plates or pie tins, and set them out for the children.

Tip: The soap in the paint helps with cleanup, but not if you use red. Red is almost impossible to wash out.

What to Do

1. Explain to the children that nature provides a lot of materials that can be used for paintbrushes. Pick up a twig, rock, or leaf and demonstrate how to dip the natural material into the paint to use it as a paintbrush on the paper or sheet.
2. Let the children gather their own natural materials to use as paintbrushes.
3. Encourage the children's experimentation by asking open-ended questions such as, "What would happen if you rolled that rock?" or "What would it look like if you laid the leaf down and pressed it with your hand?"
4. Ask the children about the colors they are using, the shapes they are making, or the patterns they see.
5. When the painting has dried, hang the children's creations in the classroom for all to enjoy.

Kay Flowers, Summerfield, OH

Fence Weaving

Learning Objectives: To explore creative thinking; to develop small motor skills

Materials

chain-link fence (Note: If you do not have a chain-link fence, you can use plastic mesh or a volleyball net.)

weaving materials—strips of fabric, ribbons, yarn, rope or twine, long grasses, twigs, crepe paper, caution tape, paper strips

What to Do

You can let this project expand over several days, depending on the children's interest.

1. Show the children some examples of weaving, such as baskets and rag rugs. Point out the over-and-under pattern of the strips of fabric or grasses.
2. Show the children how to weave materials in and out through the openings in the fence.
3. Give the children a variety of materials to work with, and let them spread out along the fence and create their own designs.
4. When the children are finished weaving, look at their creations together. What colors, patterns, and details do they notice?

Children's Books

Mayan Weaving: A Living Tradition by Ann Stalcup
Patterns by Bev Schumacher

Tip: This activity can lead naturally into a simple social studies lesson about how people around the world create weavings, or a natural history lesson about birds and their nests.

Bev Schumacher, Racine, WI and Shelley Hoster, Norcross, GA

Messy Painting Adventures

3+

Learning Objectives: To encourage creativity and group cooperation; to develop small and large motor skills

Materials
cake pans, foil pie tins, or large foam plates
clothespins
large, solid-colored sheets or large pieces of fabric
old T-shirts or smocks for the children to wear
tape
variety of clean, unusual painting tools: spray bottles, plungers, flyswatters, brooms, sponge toilet-bowl cleaners
water-based paints

Preparation
- Pour paint into the plates, pans, or pie tins.
- Using tape, secure these flat containers to prevent them from blowing away or being knocked over.
- Lay out several large pieces of fabric for the children to paint on. You will need to tape them down as well.

What to Do
1. Offer the children the painting tools.
2. Encourage them to dip the painting tools into paint and use them for painting on the fabric.
3. As they paint, ask about the colors they are using. Ask them to talk about their painting.
4. When the creation is completed, use the clothespins to hang it on a school fence to dry.
5. Look at the finished artwork with the children. What details do they notice? What colors, shapes, and patterns? What can they tell you about the painting process?
6. When the painting is dry, hang it in the classroom: perhaps as the background for a bulletin board.

Bev Schumacher, Racine, WI

Paint the Outdoors!

3+

Learning Objectives: To develop the skills of sorting, counting, and classifying; to practice small motor skills; to learn new vocabulary

Materials
bags, one per child
glitter (optional)
liquid tempera paint
paintbrushes
paper towels
sequins (optional)
tray or table
water for hand washing and rinsing brushes

Preparation
- Prepare small trays with paint (and glitter or sequins, if desired) for the children to use after their hunt.

What to Do
Cleanup is easier when you do this activity outside!
1. Give each child a bag. Take the children on a hunt for natural items. Tell them to look for fallen leaves, twigs, pinecones, pretty rocks, and so on to place into their bags.
2. When you return to the playground, ask the children to put their items onto a tray or table. They can count as they take each item out. How many leaves? How many rocks? Can they sort their items?
3. Encourage the children to decorate what they found. Let them paint on their nature finds by using their fingers or paintbrushes. (Not every child will want to decorate what they found. Some will want to take their treasures home as they are.)
4. Help the children to clean their hands when they are finished.
5. Lay the items out to dry. When they are dry, take the items back to the classroom to display in a window or on a table.

Sarah Stonebraker, Seattle, WA

Paint the Town Wet!

3+

Learning Objective: To develop small and large motor control

Materials
buckets
large paintbrushes, one for each child
warm day
water

Preparation
- Using just water, you can paint anything outdoors! Consider fences, playground equipment, brick walls, grass, trees, rocks, and the sidewalk. Decide in advance if you want the children to have free choice of what they paint or if you want to limit them to a designated area.
- Fill the buckets with water and place them near the painting area.

What to Do
1. Hand each child a paintbrush.
2. Explain to the children that they are going to "paint" with water.
3. As they paint, ask the children observe what happens to the wet surface after a few minutes. Introduce the word *evaporation*.

Related Song
(to the tune of "Here We Go 'Round the Mulberry Bush")
"We Are Going to Paint the Town"
We are going to paint the town,
Paint the town,
Paint the town,
We are going to paint the town,
Up and down.
(additional verses: *High and low; Fast and slow; Here and there*)

Kara Stokke, Maumelle, AR

Wet Chalk Art

Learning Objectives: To develop creativity and small motor skills

Materials

dark-colored 12" x 18" construction paper
plastic cups
sidewalk chalk and colored stick chalk
sidewalk or other paved surface
water

Children's Books

A Piece of Chalk by Jennifer A. Ericsson
Sidewalk Chalk: Poems of the City by Carole Boston Weatherford

Preparation

- Create an outdoor area where children can either draw on colored construction paper or draw on the sidewalk.
- Put a small amount of water into each cup.
- Place the chalk and water cups into the work space.

What to Do

1. Help the children write their names on their papers or on the sidewalk where they are drawing.
2. As they work, encourage the children to dip the tips of their chalk into the water. Chalk drawings are more brilliant and will last longer when drawn with wet chalk.
3. If the children draw on paper, hang the paper creations to dry. Set the wet chalk aside to dry for later use.
4. If the children draw directly on a sidewalk, consider taking photos of their creations. Hang the photos on a bulletin board or place them in the children's portfolios.
5. Talk with each child about the colors he is using, the shapes he is drawing, and the subjects he has chosen.

Tina R. Durham-Woehler, Lebanon, TN

4+

Art Stations

Learning Objectives: To encourage creativity; to explore tools and media; to develop small and large motor skills

Materials
easels that can be set up outdoors
materials to paint on, such as aluminum foil, butcher paper, brown paper bags, construction paper, and fabric
materials to paint with, such as paint rollers and paintbrushes
natural materials, such as branches, sticks, leaves, rocks, and grass
paints, such as liquid tempera paints in varying thicknesses and colors and watercolors
scissors
smocks or old T-shirts, one for each child
zipper-seal plastic bags

Children's Book
The Artist Who Painted a Blue Horse by Eric Carle
I Am an Artist by Pat Lowery Collins
Lily Brown's Paintings by Angela Johnson
The Magical Garden of Claude Monet by Laurence Anholt

Tip: Take a picture of each artist creating so that you can display the photos by their masterpieces.

Preparation
* Set up stations where the children can explore different art media.
  For example, you could set up a station for painting with natural materials, one for painting onto aluminum foil, one with plastic bags filled with paint (cut a tiny hole in one corner, so the paint can be squeezed out), and a station for painting onto fabric.
* Mark off an area where the children can place their finished artwork to dry.

What to Do
Allow plenty of time for this activity. You may want to set it up several days in a row so that all the children can explore each station that interests them.
1. Talk with the children about artists and what they do. Describe how artists use different tools to create their artwork.
2. Read a story about an artist, and show the children examples of that artist's work.
3. Take the children around to the different art stations, explaining what the materials are and how to use them.
4. Let each child choose a station, or consider assigning the children to different stations.
5. After a child has finished exploring at one station, encourage him to place his art in the drying spot and then to move to another station and create a new masterpiece.

Holly Dzierzanowski, Bastrop, TX

Families Totally Rock!

Learning Objectives: To develop small motor skills; to increase vocabulary about family relationships; to develop counting skills

Materials
boxes or bags (optional)
fine-point permanent marker
sandpaper
scrap wood squares or rectangles, one for each child
small, flat rocks
water
white glue

Preparation
- Sand any rough edges from the wood scraps.
- Have all the materials except the rocks in a place where the children can do this project directly on the ground or on a large sheet outside.

What to Do
1. Read some books about families, and talk with the children about their own families. Some children may not live in traditional family units.
2. Help the children count how many people are in their families.
3. Take the children outside where they can gather small, flat rocks. The children may put them in their pockets or carry them in a box or bag. Explain that they will need to gather as many rocks as they have people in their individual families. Help each child count how many rocks he will need.
4. Let the children wash the rocks and lay them out to dry.
5. When each child is ready, help him glue selected clean rocks onto the wood scraps, labeling each rock with the name of a family member. Help as needed.
6. Let the projects dry overnight, and then let the children take their projects home.

Children's Books
Families Are Special by
 Norma Simon
Foster Families by
 Sarah L. Schuette
If You Find a Rock by
 Peggy Christian
My Family Is Forever by
 Nancy Carlson
A Wild Father's Day by
 Sean Callahan

Tip: These make unique gifts for Father's Day, Mother's Day, or Grandparents Day.

Kay Flowers, Summerfield, OH

Shadow Painting

Learning Objectives: To learn to follow simple directions; to develop small and large motor skills

Materials

brushes
bucket of water for rinsing
large sheet of paper for each child
outdoor area with shadows from trees, playground equipment, street signs, and so on
portable cups of tempera paints placed into a shoebox
rocks or heavy objects to hold down the corners of the paper
sunny day
towel

Children's Books

Lights Out! Shadow Pop Up and Play by Richard Fowler
Moonbear's Shadow by Frank Asch
Shadow by Suzy Lee
Shadows and Reflections by Tana Hoban

Preparation

• Fill paint cups half full and place into the shoebox for portable transport outdoors.
• Fill a bucket half full with water for portable outdoor rinsing of brushes.
• You may need rocks or weighted objects to hold down the corners of the large sheets of paper so it will not blow away.

What to Do

1. Find a shadow on the ground—perhaps of a tree or of a friend standing still.
2. Spread the large sheet of paper on the ground to capture part of the shadow.
3. Look at the shadow on the paper. Paint the shadow in any way you choose: Paint inside the shadow shape, or paint around the shadow.
4. Leave the painting to dry in place, or carry the painting indoors to dry.

Tip: It will be a teaching and discovery moment if you leave the paper in place to dry on the ground. When you return to it later, the child can see that the shadow has moved and the shape has changed.

MaryAnn F. Kohl, Bellingham, WA

Chapter 6: The Sense of Touch

The outdoors is a perfect setting for explorations using the sense of touch. Interesting textures are everywhere. Use the activities in this chapter to focus the children's attention on using their sense of touch, but you will also want to let the children explore and discover on their own.

3+

Mud Play

Learning Objectives: To learn texture vocabulary and expressive language; to practice small motor skills

Children's Books
Mud Puddle by Robert Munsch
Mud Tacos by Mario Lopez and Marissa Lopez Wong

Materials

dirt (Note: Do not use commercial potting soil, as some potting soils contain chemicals and additives that can be harmful to children.)

empty, clean pie pans

plastic dishwashing tubs

plastic plates and serving utensils

plastic tablecloth

sand molds

scoops, shovels, spoons

smocks or old T-shirts

water

Preparation

- Find an outdoor space where children can use dirt and water to make mud.
- If needed, spread a plastic tablecloth over the work space to allow for easy cleanup and surface protection.
- Place dirt into some of the tubs, and place spoons, scoops, and so on into the dirt.
- Pour water into another plastic tub for children to scoop out to mix with the dirt and make mud.

What to Do

1. Have the children put on smocks or T-shirts before play begins.
2. If necessary, show the children how to add water to the dirt to make mud. Let them explore the texture of the mud, squishing it between their fingers and smashing it in their hands.
3. Show them how to form mud pies by packing the mud into the pie pans. Let them experiment with how much water to add to the dirt to get the right consistency for mud pies.
4. To expand into dramatic play, encourage the children to "serve" the mud pies to each other on plastic plates. What pretend food have they made? Birthday cake? apple pie? Maybe another favorite dessert? What else can they create from the mud?
5. When the children have finished exploring the mud, help them wash their hands and rinse off the muddy toys.

Tina R. Durham-Woehler, Lebanon, TN

Surfboard Feet

Learning Objectives: To discriminate between *dry* and *wet, squishy* and *rough;* to practice balance and other large motor skills

Materials
2–3 buckets
butcher paper (any color)
liquid dish detergent
liquid tempera paint in a variety of colors
sand
scissors
towels
trays
warm day
water

What to Do
1. Roll out several sheets of butcher paper onto the grass or onto pavement. If desired, cut the paper into the shape of a surfboard.
2. Pour paint into trays that are large enough for little feet to dip into. Mix in a few drops of liquid dish detergent to make cleanup easier. Add a little sand to the paint to create an interesting texture. (Note: Red is hard to wash out, even with detergent mixed in, so use caution!)
3. Encourage the children to dip their feet into the trays of paint! (Note: The trays will be slippery, so be sure to help them.)
4. Help the children walk onto the paper. They can make "waves" with their feet or any pattern they choose.
5. Help the children dip their feet into the water to wash off, and dry their feet with the towels.

Tip: You can make this part of an imaginative exploration of the beach. Set it up near the sand area and include beach towels and other props: beach chairs, shovels, shells, buckets, and a source of water. Eat snacks or lunch outside for a beach picnic.

Sarah Stonebraker, Seattle, WA

Feely Numbers

Learning Objective: To practice number recognition and counting

Materials

sets of numbers 1–9 made of wood or plastic

small paper bags, one for each child

strong, opaque bag, big enough for two hands to move around inside

What to Do

1. Fill the large bag with the wood or plastic numbers from 1 to 9. If the children are just beginning to learn numbers, use only two or three different numbers at a time, but have lots of them.
2. Tell the children that they are going to play a number game. First, they will put their hands inside the bag and pick out just one number. Then, with their hands still inside the bag, they must feel the number with both hands, and tell everyone what number they think it is. Then, they will pull it out and show everyone.
3. Pass the bag around the circle, and give each child a turn to pick out a number, feel it, and make a guess.
4. When everyone has picked and guessed a number, pass out the paper bags and write each child's number on her bag.
5. At the word, "Go!" let the children race around the play area and gather up the appropriate number of objects to put into their bags. Help as needed.
6. When everyone has found the right number of objects, they can dump out their bags to see what they have, count the objects, and use them in any play scenario they choose.

Anne Adeney, Plymouth, UK

Hand Sand Castings

Learning Objective: To become familiar with the terms *liquid* and *solid* and recognize the difference between them

Materials

damp sand

measuring cups and spoons

paper bags (optional)

paper cups

plaster of Paris

plastic spoons

shallow plastic tub

water

Preparation

- Place damp sand into a shallow tub and pat it down firmly. (Note: For large groups, use multiple tubs or a sandbox.)

What to Do

1. Working with small groups of children, guide each child to press one hand firmly into the damp sand to make a handprint.
2. Following the package instructions, measure plaster of Paris into a paper cup.
3. Measure the proper amount of water and add that to the cup of plaster. Allow the child to help stir with a plastic spoon.
4. Encourage the children to notice the consistency of the plaster mixed with water—it is a liquid. It flows and takes the shape of the container it is in.
5. Help each child pour the liquefied plaster into her hand impression.
6. After approximately 30–45 minutes (see package instructions) the castings should have hardened. Allow each child gently to lift her hand shape gently from the sand. (Some sand will remain embedded in the plaster.)
7. Ask the children to describe how the plaster has changed. It is now a solid. It does not change shape but is compact and hard.

Tip: Completed castings may be placed in your school garden as decorative pieces or sent home. If sending the castings home, place each into a bag so any loose sand will not cause a mess.

Rob Sanders, Brandon, FL

THE SENSE OF TOUCH

Rock Collecting

Learning Objectives: To develop observation skills and language skills; to practice classifying objects by size, shape, and other attributes

Materials

newspaper
paintbrushes
paper towels
small cups
sturdy bags for collecting
tempera paint
water

Children's Books

Everybody Needs a Rock by
    Byrd Baylor
If You Find a Rock by
    Peggy Christian
Rocks and Minerals by
    DK Publishing

What to Do

1. Give the children bags and encourage them to look for rocks to collect during an outdoor walk.
2. When everyone has found several rocks they like, ask them to bring them back to the group. Let them show their discoveries.
3. Discuss the shapes, sizes, and colors of the rocks they found. Compare the sizes, textures, colors, and shapes of the rocks and stones.
4. Let the children wash and dry their rocks.
5. If necessary, spread out newspaper to protect the painting surface.
6. Give the children paint in cups and paintbrushes. Let the children paint their rocks any way they choose.
7. Set the rocks in a safe place to dry.

Jean Potter, Greensburg, PA

Rough or Smooth

Learning Objectives: To practice identifying textures as *rough* or *smooth*; to record the results

Materials
clipboard
paper
pencil
sandpaper

Children's Books
Is It Rough? Is It Smooth? Is It Shiny? by Tana Hoban
Spiky, Slimy, Smooth: What Is Texture? by Jane Brocket

Preparation
- Scout out a variety of textured surfaces, such as a brick wall, tree bark, sidewalk, fence post, sign, leaves, door, glass, and other surfaces that will be rough or smooth.
- Make a T chart on a piece of paper to record the children's findings. Label one side *rough* and the other side *smooth*.

What to Do
1. Explain that *texture* means "how the surface of an object feels to the touch." Ask the children to rub their faces to feel something smooth. Then ask them to feel the sandpaper to see how *rough* feels.
2. Walk around and find a texture, such as a brick wall. Ask the children to close their eyes and feel the wall. Does it feel smooth like the skin on their faces or rough like the sandpaper?
3. When they have decided, write the name of the object on the clipboard under the correct heading, and add a simple drawing to help the children remember what the object was.
4. Repeat with another texture to feel and label as either *rough* or *smooth*.
5. When your class texture search is complete, look at the T chart with the children and recall the different textures they discovered. Are there more rough objects or more smooth objects?

Susan Oldham Hill, Lakeland, FL

Sensory Walk

Learning Objectives: To develop sensory awareness; to practice descriptive language

Children's Books
The Foot Book by Dr. Seuss
My Five Senses by Aliki

Materials

1½ cups water
3 cups cornstarch
7 plastic tubs big enough for
　stepping into
bubble wrap
cotton balls
dry leaves
sand
soapy water
Styrofoam "peanuts"
towels

Preparation

- Mix up the oobleck (cornstarch and water) in a tub. Place this tub next to last, just before the soapy water tub.
- Fill the rest of the tubs with the different items, then line up the tubs in a row.
- Put the tub with the soapy water at the end of the line, along with a towel. This way after the children have walked through the tubs, they can wash their feet and dry off at the end.

What to Do

1. Read a book with the children about the five senses, and talk about how we use our senses to learn about the world.
2. Show the children the different tubs and talk about the contents of each. Ask them to guess what they think each substance will feel and sound like.
3. Help the children take off their shoes and socks in preparation for walking in the tubs. (Note: Not all children will be willing to put their feet into the tubs. If they prefer, they can put their hands into the tubs instead, or just watch the other children as they walk through the tubs.) Line up the shoes and socks at the end of the tubs for them to put on when they are done with the walk.
4. Let the children walk through the tubs and tell you how each thing feels on their feet. Have them describe which senses they are using. For example, when they go through the bubble wrap, they will hear the pop with their ears and feel the bubbles with the sense of touch.

Tip: If you walk through the tubs first yourself, talk about how it feels to you, and show the children how to do it; the reluctant ones may be encouraged to try it themselves.

Holly Dzierzanowski, Bastrop, TX

Texture Rubbings

Learning Objectives: To learn about texture; to begin to use words to describe various textures

Materials
crayons
lightweight paper
masking tape
pencils
scissors
stapler

Preparation
- Cut the paper into sheets approximately 5½" x 8".
- Remove the wrappers from the crayons.

What to Do
1. Explain to the children that the word *texture* means, "how something feels to the touch." For example, wet soap is *slippery,* your skin is *smooth,* and a tree trunk is *rough.*
2. Demonstrate how to do a texture rubbing. First, run your hand over the textured item (for example: a picnic table, a sidewalk, or a leaf). Describe what you feel to the children. Use texture words. Next, tape a piece of paper on top of the textured surface. Gently rub the side of a crayon or a pencil over the surface until an image of the texture appears.
3. Encourage the children to look for interesting textures. Give them paper and crayons, and help them make rubbings of the textures they discover.
4. When the children have finished making their texture rubbings, ask them to describe the way each texture feels with a word or two. Write the word(s) below each rubbing.
5. As they work, ask the children to talk about the textures they find. Can different things have similar textures? Can the same thing have more than one texture?
6. Collect the sheets, stack them together, and staple them along one edge to form a class texture book.

Tip: Keep the book in your classroom library for future use and reference.

Rob Sanders, Brandon, FL, and Jean Potter, Greensburg, PA

Rubbing Safari

Learning Objectives: To learn about textures found in nature; to practice following a map

Materials

crayon

leaves

paper

several plastic flying discs, 12" x 12" squares of cardboard, or other sturdy markers to place on the ground

Children's Books

Smooth or Rough by Charlotte Guillain

What Is Texture? by Stephanie Fitzgerald

Preparation

- Make rubbings of several items in the schoolyard: tree bark, a smooth stone, a leaf, and so on.
- Place a 12" x 12" marker next to each item.
- Make a simple map of the schoolyard, marking each place where you made a rubbing.

What to Do

1. Show the children how to make a leaf rubbing, and let each child try it.
2. Discuss what the rubbing shows: the outline and the texture of the leaf.
3. Show them the rubbings you made. Explain that they are to find each of the items from which you made rubbings.
4. Show them the map, and explain that it shows where each rubbing was made. If they stand at the marker and look around, they will be able to find what the rubbing shows.
5. Pair up the children, and encourage them to work together to follow the map. Guide them as needed until they find all of the items.

Sue Bradford Edwards, Florissant, MO

Texture Scavenger Hunt

Learning Objective: To practice identifying textures

Materials

crayon
materials to use for demonstration (shiny, rough, etc.)
paper
scavenger hunt lists

Children's Books

Is It Rough? Is It Smooth? Is It Shiny? by Tana Hoban
Spiky, Slimy, Smooth: What Is Texture? by Jane Brocket
What Is Texture? by Stephanie Fitzgerald

Preparation

- Gather a variety of materials to use for demonstration. Make sure to have several types of textures: bumpy, smooth, rough, striated (lined), and so on.
- Create a scavenger hunt list consisting of pictures of a variety of textures. For example, you might include things such as one small, smooth object (a smooth stone); one large, rough object (a tree trunk); something large and smooth (the bed of a slide might be one example); and three letters (company names stamped on play equipment).

What to Do

1. Ask the children if anyone knows what the word *texture* means. Allow time for answers and a brief discussion that *texture* means "how something feels to the touch."
2. Show the children a variety of textured objects. As you show each object, ask several children to touch it and describe its texture.
3. Demonstrate how to make a rubbing. Label it with the agreed-upon texture words. Continue until all the demonstration items have been used.
4. Tell the children they will be going on a scavenger hunt for textures in the schoolyard. They can use your examples to identify textures if they need to.
5. Pair up the children and hand out scavenger hunt lists, paper, and crayons.
6. Encourage them to find and make a rubbing of each item on their list. Offer help as needed. As the children finish, collect the rubbings for display in the classroom.

Tip: Rubbings can be cut up and used to create interesting collages or greeting cards.

Kathryn Hake, Lebanon, OR

LET'S TAKE IT OUTSIDE

Chapter 7: Sound and Sight

The activities in this chapter help children focus on the sense of sight and the sense of hearing. These two senses give us essential information about our environment. When you are outside, occasionally ask children to stop and listen, and then tell you what they hear. What stories are the sounds telling?

Let's Listen!

Learning Objective: To practice recognizing outdoor sounds

Materials
outdoor area
recording device (optional)
towels or blankets to sit on

What to Do

1. As you sit together on the blankets or towels, read a book about sounds and hearing.
2. Tell the children they are going to use their sense of hearing to explore the sounds around them. To get them started, list a few sounds they might hear: birds chirping, leaves rustling, a squirrel scampering up a tree, a lawn mower, people talking, cars and trucks, and so on. Ask the children to add to the list.
3. Now, ask the children to sit very quietly and listen for lots of different sounds. When a child hears a sound, he should raise his hand. Encourage children to share one by one the sounds they hear.
4. If desired, record the sounds you hear and play them back later for the children. Do they notice any sounds on the recording that they did not notice when they were outside?

Children's Books
Perk Up Your Ears: Discover Your Sense of Hearing by Vicki Cobb
Shhh . . . A Book About Hearing by Dana Meachen Rau
What Is Hearing? by Jennifer Boothroyd

Tip: Listening with your eyes closed can also be fun. Do the children hear better without the distraction of sight?

Donna Alice Patton, Hillsboro, OH

Musical Tree

Learning Objectives: To develop listening skills by differentiating among sounds; to learn to distinguish sounds of varying pitch; to develop expressive language skills

Children's Books

All About Sound by
   Lisa Trumbauer
*Sound: Loud, Soft, High, and
   Low* by Natalie Rosinsky
Sounds All Around by
   Wendy Pfeffer
Zin! Zin! Zin! A Violin by
   Lloyd Moss

Materials

kitchen tools, such as metal pots, pans, lids, and wooden or
   metal spoons
lengths of sturdy string or nylon rope

Preparation

- Gather a variety of kitchen items.
- Attach varying lengths of string or rope to the handles of the kitchen items.
- Select a suitable tree in the playground, and hang the items from the branches. Position the wooden or metal spoons near the pots, pans and lids, or attach the spoons directly to the pans and lids. (The children will be using them as strikers.)

What to Do

1. Read a book about sounds. Talk with the children about the sounds they hear every day.
2. Encourage the children to experiment with making different sounds by using the spoons to hit the items hanging in the tree.
3. Ask them to listen carefully and compare how the different items sound. Does the smaller pot make a higher sound than the big pan? Does the pot lid sound different from the baking pan?
4. Ask them to experiment with hitting the pans quickly and slowly. Explain that the speed at which they hit the pans is called a tempo.
5. Can the children make up songs to go with their tree music?

Tip: If possible, leave the items in the tree for the children to explore over and over again. Encourage the children to expand the collection over time and to experiment with more sounds.

**Anne Houghton,
Victoria, Australia**

4+

Binocular Fun

Learning Objective: To explore and observe the outdoors; to develop small motor skills

Materials

cardboard tubes from paper-towel rolls (2 per child)
crayons
markers
masking tape
paper

Children's Books

Brown Bear, Brown Bear, What Do You See? by Bill Martin Jr.
The Eye Book by Dr. Seuss
Fish Eyes by Lois Ehlert
Look Book by Tana Hoban
Panda Bear, Panda Bear, What Do You See? by Bill Martin Jr.

What to Do

1. Help the children make their own play binoculars by taping two cardboard tubes together side by side.
2. They can decorate their binoculars with the markers any way they wish.
3. After the binoculars are finished, walk around with the children and encourage them to look at the world through their binoculars. Do trees, grass, playground equipment, leaves, or bugs look different through the binoculars?
4. When they are finished exploring, give them paper and crayons and ask them to draw a picture of something they observed. Encourage them to dictate captions for their drawings.

Tip: Let the children use their binoculars in all kinds of imaginative free play outdoors. For example, if you read a story about explorers, you will find them creating their own exploration dramas using binoculars to find their way over the mountains. Read a story about pirates, and the binoculars will become spyglasses, and so on.

Sandy L. Scott, Meridian, ID

Close Your Eyes and Listen

Learning Objective: To think about the sense of sight and how we depend upon it

Children's Book
Through Grandpa's Eyes by Patricia MacLachlan

Materials
blindfold
noisemakers (bell, rattle, drum, horn)

What to Do

1. Gather the children together outdoors and ask them to close their eyes and listen as you talk and walk around. Ask the children if they can tell where you are standing just by the sound of your voice.

2. Discuss the words *blind* and *blindfold,* and talk about what it might be like to be blind.

3. Ask one of the children to volunteer to wear a blindfold, and help him walk around the group of children as the other children watch. Ask the blindfolded child to describe how he feels as he walks.

4. Ask other children to stand in different places and give them each a noisemaker. Ask each child in turn to make a noise and ask the blindfolded child to point to the child making the noise.

5. Continue the activity to give all the children who are interested a turn to experience being blindfolded.

Tip: You might try this activity both indoors and outdoors. Is it easier to tell where the sound is coming from when you are inside? Outside? Are there more sounds when you are inside or when you are outside? Are the sounds different?

Kimberley Barnes, Burnettsville, IN

Color Telescopes

Learning Objective: To learn how mixing two colors creates a new color

Materials

cardboard tubes from paper-towel rolls (one per child)
colored cellophane in red, yellow, and blue
markers
rubber bands
scissors

Children's Books

Color Dance by Ann Jonas
Planting a Rainbow by
   Lois Ehlert

What to Do

1. Cut cellophane into 5" squares.
2. The children can decorate their paper-towel rolls with markers however they would like.
3. Suggest that the children take pieces of colored cellophane and look through them. What do they see?
4. Encourage the children to try the colored cellophane pieces alone and in various combinations. Encourage the children to talk about the colors they see and to share their discoveries with one another.
5. Let each child choose the cellophane colors that make the color he wants for his telescope. Show the children how to hold these pieces over one end of the tube and secure them with a rubber band. Help as needed with this step.
6. Encourage children to look through one another's telescopes and to take their color telescopes outside to look at nature through the colored lenses.

Judith Dighe, Rockville, MD

Four Seasons of Nature Walks

Learning Objectives: To observe the changing seasons; to use descriptive language; to practice small motor skills

Materials
digital camera
glue
paper lunch bags
poster board

Children's Books
Four Seasons Make a Year by
   Anne Rockwell
Our Seasons by
   Ranida T. McKneally
The Reasons for Seasons by
   Gail Gibbons
*The Seasons of Arnold's Apple
   Tree* by Gail Gibbons

What to Do

1. Read a book or two about how each season is different. If you live in an area where the seasons do not change dramatically, supplement the books with photographs depicting seasonal changes, and discuss how the seasons in your area may be different from what is depicted in some books.
2. Pick one day of each season to do a collecting nature walk with the children. Talk ahead of time about what you may observe on the nature walk. For example, will you see flowers in bloom? Will the air be warm or cold? Will there be green leaves on the trees? What smells do you expect to notice? What sounds? Will you see any animals or insects?
3. Give each child a paper bag, and encourage each to collect items that show what the season is. (Note: Do not pick living plants or gather living insects or animals.) Take photos of items that you cannot pick or gather. For example, in autumn, the children could collect fallen leaves. In spring, they can take photos of flowers or butterflies. In the winter, they might collect a leafless twig or take a photo of an ice crystal.
4. After returning to the room, look at the collection of items the children have gathered and print the pictures. Talk with the children about the details they noticed on the walk.
5. Create a poster collage with the pictures and items. Date the collage and label it with the season.
6. As the seasons change, take additional nature walks and hang each new collage near the first seasonal collage.

Sandy L. Scott, Meridian, ID

I Am the Outdoors!

Learning Objectives: To practice following directions; to develop observation and language skills

Materials

What to Do

1. Gather the children together outdoors and ask them to look around and name some of the things they see.

2. Play a game in which each person pretends to be something you see. First, give some information about your choice, maybe by creating a little chant. For example, you might say, "I am the sky, and I'm very, very high." Then you might stand on tiptoes and reach your arms high over your head to demonstrate. Or, "I am a flower, and I'm very, very pretty!"

3. Let each child name something he sees, tell a bit of information about that thing, and then act out what he sees.

Tip: There are many opportunities for active movement and imagination with this game. Get creative and ask the children show how the wind would blow them if they were trees. Encourage the children to stand up straight and tall, like the grass, or to flap their wings like the birds. Tell the children to "be" whatever they see!

Jan Black, San Francisco, CA

Name That Voice

Learning Objectives: To develop careful listening; to practice following directions

Children's Book
The Listening Walk by Paul Showers

Materials
blindfold

What to Do
This game can be played anywhere, indoors or out.

1. Have the children sit in a circle, and tell them that they will play a game in which they will try to identify each other by voice and one simple clue. (Children may stand if it is muddy or wet.)
2. Ask one child to close his eyes and cover them with his hands or to wear a blindfold.
3. Point to another child. This child gently taps the first child on the back, and identifies himself by saying, "Hi. I have _____." (Mention something that describes the child, such as brown hair, blue eyes, a green sweater, and so on.) This child then returns to his place in the circle.
4. The first child uncovers his eyes and tries to guess which child spoke to him. The other children can give additional clues if necessary.
5. The second child then becomes the next one to cover his eyes.

Nancy L. Schwider, Glen Elyn, IL

SOUND AND SIGHT

Picnic Snatcher

Learning Objective: To identify a missing item removed from a group of objects

Materials
5–10 small objects gathered from your play kitchen
basket
blanket

Children's Books
The Teddy Bears' Picnic by Jimmy Kennedy (several other versions are available)

What to Do

1. Gather the children around the blanket in a comfortable grassy area. Read *The Teddy Bears' Picnic* or simply tell an imaginary story about going on a picnic in the woods where teddy bears live.
2. Take a few of the objects out of the basket. Ask the children to name each item as you set it onto the blanket.
3. Pretend that you are sharing a wonderful meal but then suddenly feel sleepy. Ask the children to bow their heads and close their eyes as if they are feeling very drowsy.
4. Quickly hide an object under the blanket and say, "Oh no, wake up! We've just been invaded by a picnic snatcher! Those mischievous little teddy bears! Can you guess what's missing?"
5. Encourage the children's responses. If they have difficulty guessing which item is missing, ask them to name the items they see. Someone will may remember the name of the missing item.
6. Repeat the game and gradually increase its difficulty by placing more items on the blanket and rearranging the objects.

Tip: This guessing game could be incorporated into any number of outdoor play scenarios. Play it with toy cars, trucks, sand tools, or any other material you have outdoors.

Susan Arentson Sharkey, Fletcher Hills, CA

Sound Lotto

Learning Objective: To identify different outdoor sounds and match them with photos

Materials

camera, if possible
clear contact paper or laminating machine
glue
old magazines to use as a source of pictures
poster board
sound recorder

What to Do

1. Engage the children in a discussion about listening and sounds.
2. Take a walk around the school grounds or around the neighborhood, listening for different sounds.
3. Record the sounds you hear: water running, leaves rustling, people talking, dogs barking, and so on.
4. Take a photograph or find a magazine picture of everything you record. Make two sets of pictures.
5. Make a lotto board using one set of pictures.
6. Glue the extra pictures onto cards and cover everything with clear contact paper or laminate.
7. Go outside again with the lotto board and a device to play back the recorded sounds.
8. Have children listen to sounds and match the pictures on the cards to the pictures on the lotto board.

Tip: Let this activity be a springboard into conversations about outdoor sounds whenever you are outside.

Audrey Kanoff, Bethlehem, PA

4+

What Is It?

Learning Objectives: To learn to discriminate without using the sense of sight; to develop descriptive language and critical thinking

Children's Book
Knots on a Counting Rope by
Bill Martin Jr. and
John Archambault

Materials
blindfolds
jump rope (optional)
various outdoor objects

What to Do

1. Talk with the children about how they can identify objects by feeling them with their hands, even when they cannot see the objects.
2. Ask a child to put on a blindfold. Hand him an object found outside (rock, leaf, piece of bark), and ask him to guess what it is.
3. Continue until all the children have had a turn.
4. Ask the children to describe how they identified the objects. Discuss using shape, size, and texture as clues.

Tip: To expand on the idea of experiencing the world without using your sense of sight, you can blindfold one or two children and ask them to hold onto a jump rope. Lead them slowly around the playground, letting them tell you what they notice. Keep the walk short. Was this hard? Was it a little scary? Talk about the experience when you are finished.

Melissa Browning, West Allis, WI

Magnify It

Learning Objectives: To learn how to use a magnifying glass; to draw, write, or dictate observations

Children's Books
Miffy's Magnifying Glass by
   Dick Bruna
You Can Use a Magnifying Glass by Wiley Blevins

Materials
magnifying glasses (one for each pair of children)
paper
pencils

What to Do

1. Talk about what it means to *observe* and to make *observations*. Explain that a magnifying glass is a tool for making careful observations. Magnifying glasses make small things appear larger. Show the children a magnifying glass and how to use it. Demonstrate how you may have to move it closer to the object or farther away in order to see clearly.
2. Pair up the children and give each pair a magnifying glass to share.
3. Encourage the pairs to explore the area and to choose one thing in the environment to observe, such as the bark of a tree or the grass.
4. Help the children focus their attention and to describe their observations. Do they see bumps on leaves they thought were smooth? Are the ants carrying food? Does the silk of a spiderweb shimmer in the breeze?
5. After the children have explored for a while, ask them to return to an area where they can draw.
6. Hand out paper and pencils, and ask the children to draw one thing, first as it looked without the magnifying glass, then as it looked through the magnifying glass.
7. Let them dictate descriptions of their drawings for you to write down.
8. Collect the drawings and make a class book about observations through magnifying glasses.

Tip: You do not need a garden or field for this activity. You will find plenty to look at in any open outdoor space.

Debbie Vilardi, Commack, NY

LET'S TAKE IT OUTSIDE

Chapter 8: Plants and Gardening

Plants are endlessly fascinating; they teach incomparable lessons about growth and change. Gardening is a natural activity for children. From making compost to planting a tree on the playground, children can be involved and engaged every step of the way.

A Bunny Rabbit's Garden

Learning Objectives: To develop imaginative thinking and descriptive language; to increase small and large motor skills; to learn about the cycle of plant growth

Children's Books
Beatrix Potter: The Complete Tales
by Beatrix Potter

Materials

9" x 12" craft foam sheets

any of the tales by Beatrix Potter, especially *The Tale of Peter Rabbit*

clear packing tape

garden plot or planters and soil

permanent colored markers

rakes, shovels, small garden stakes

scissors

vegetable seeds (as described below)

water

Preparation

- Select some of the following vegetable seed packets that correspond with the plants mentioned in the story of Peter Rabbit: lettuces, beans, radishes, parsley, cucumbers, cabbages, potatoes, peas, and onions.
- Gather the necessary garden tools.
- Select a spot for your garden. If a spot is not available, use large planters that you can place in a sunny spot.

What to Do

1. Read the story aloud. Explain that Peter will be able to stay out of trouble with his neighbor, Mr. McGregor, if we plant a garden for him to call his own.
2. Cut the craft foam sheets in half to make markers for the seed rows. Help the children print vegetable names and illustrate the markers.
3. Trim the markers around the edges of the designs. Fasten the markers to stakes with tape.
4. Start the planting process according to the directions provided on the seed packets. When each seed packet is empty, attach it to the appropriate marker.
5. Place the markers to identify each row of seeds.
6. Observe, tend, and water the seeds and young plants.
7. When the produce is ready, pick and enjoy the vegetables that grow in your Bunny Garden.

Tip: Keep a garden log, and record your observations and the children's comments about the planting and growth processes.

**Susan Arentson Sharkey,
Fletcher Hills, CA**

Digging in the Dirt

Learning Objectives: To improve coordination and large motor skills; to identify various yard and garden tools to enhance vocabulary

Materials

children's gardening tools such as rakes, shovels, and trowels
gardening apparel such as gloves, sun hats, garden clogs, or boots
outdoor area where children can dig in the dirt (Use a sandbox
  if necessary.)

What to Do

1. Gather the children near the plot of soil or sandbox. Read aloud a book about gardening, such as *Tools for the Garden* by Mari C. Schuh.

2. Talk about how tools make gardening and yard work easier. Show the children the tools, identify them by name, and demonstrate their use.

3. Display some of the gardening apparel you could wear as you work in the garden. Demonstrate how to wear the gloves, garden clogs or boots, and the gardening hat, and talk about how they protect your body while working outdoors.

4. Let the children explore the tools and apparel, using them as they dig in the dirt!

Children's Books:
Lenny in the Garden by
  Ken Wilson-Max
Our Generous Garden by
  Ann Nagro
Tools for the Garden by
  Mari C. Schuh

Tip: If a neighbor near your school has a garden, ask if you can bring the class over for an exploratory field trip about soil and gardening.

Mary Murray, Mazomanie, WI

4+

Planting a Tree

Learning Objectives: To cultivate an attitude of sharing and working together; to develop large motor skills

Materials

fertilizer (check with your plant nursery about what is needed and
   what is safe for children to handle)
hoses, watering cans, and water
shovels for adults and children
small tree to plant

Children's Books

Be a Friend to Trees by
   Patricia Lauber
*Planting the Trees of Kenya: The
   Story of Wangari Maathai* by
   Claire A. Nivola
Tell Me, Tree by Gail Gibbons
We Planted a Tree by
   Diane Muldrow

Preparation

- Pick out the piece of ground where you will plant the tree.
- Prepare the soil by loosening the dirt so it will be easy enough for children to use the shovels.
- Select a tree recommended for your area. The young tree should be small, preferably no taller than the height of the children.

What to Do

1. Talk about trees with the children. What do they know about them? Read a book about trees. Explain that trees are important because they provide shade, oxygen, homes for animals, and food for animals and for people.
2. Tell the children that they will plant their very own class tree. Tell them there will be a variety of jobs, such as digging a hole with shovels, placing fertilizer in the hole, placing the tree in the hole, shoveling in dirt, and watering.
3. Assign jobs to the children and pass out the appropriate tools.
4. Work together to plant, fertilize, and water your tree.
5. Take a picture of the children with their tree. As time passes, visit the tree often, making sure it is watered and noticing how it is changing. Take photos on each visit.

Tip: Make a chart on which you record the changes in the tree over time. Measure its height and circumference, and note any changes in the leaves.

**Shirley Anne Ramaley,
Sun City, AZ**

A Beautiful Tree

Learning Objective: To practice close observation and vocabulary by drawing trees and naming the parts of a tree

Children's Books
Our Tree Named Steve by Alan Zweibel
Tell Me, Tree by Gail Gibbons
A Tree Is Nice by Janice May Udry

Materials
clipboards
crayons
drawing paper

Preparation
• Collect clipboards or other firm drawing surfaces, one for each child

What to Do
1. Read stories, look at pictures, and discuss trees. Point out trunks, leaves, branches, roots, and how the sun shines through the leaves. Discuss the colors: not all leaves are green, and not all trunks are brown.
2. Look closely at the trunks of several trees. Ask the children to name all the colors they can see on the bark. Talk about the way the branches extend from the trunk.
3. Give each child a clipboard, and pair up the children to share crayons. Ask the pairs to find a tree to sit by and to draw. (**Note:** When the children have worked for a while and feel they are finished, name the parts they have included and ask, "What else could you add?")
4. Collect the children's drawings for display on a bulletin board or in a class book

Susan Oldham Hill, Lakeland, FL

Compost Heap

Learning Objectives: To learn how to make compost; to discover how compost keeps the earth healthy

Materials

bucket

food scraps (no meat; avoid dairy products)

grass clippings

large, bottomless container for the compost bin (**Tip:** You can create your own compost bin by forming chicken wire or lightweight fencing into a circle.)

leaves

magnifying glasses

outside space

pitchfork or shovel

Children's Books

Compost Stew by
  Mary McKenna Siddals
Yucky Worms by Vivian French

Preparation

- Set up the compost bin outdoors before beginning this project with the children.
- Gather some fallen leaves and some grass clippings.
- Put the leaves and grass clippings into the bottom of the compost container.

What to Do

1. Talk to the children about different things we can do with food leftovers and with the scraps that remain after we have prepared food for a snack or meal. Explain that food scraps can be used to make compost.
2. Explain to the children that compost is healthy for the earth. When leftover food is put into a compost heap and is left to settle over many months, worms and other small animals and bacteria in the soil break down the plant matter, and it becomes reusable as soil.

3. Collect food scraps after lunch or snack time each day and place them into the pail. (Fruit and vegetable peels, bread crusts and coffee grounds are particularly useful. Avoid all animal products.) Go out to the compost heap and add the scraps to the bin. Cover them with a layer of soil, leaves, or grass clippings.

4. Every week, turn the contents of the compost heap with a pitchfork or shovel. It is okay to let it get wet in the rain. If it does not rain, you should water it occasionally. Layer the heap with leaves, scraps, soil, and grass clippings if you have them. Keep repeating this layering.

5. Periodically take out a shovelful of compost and look at it carefully. What do the children notice? Do they see worms? What else?

6. Over many months the scraps will gradually turn into black, crumbly soil. When the compost has fully "cooked," let the children examine it with magnifying glasses. How has it changed?

Tip: Use this compost to enrich the soil in a small garden plot. Help the children plant a small garden.

Maureen Webster, Stillwater, MN

Compost Tea

Learning Objectives: To develop observation skills and large motor skills; to become aware of and begin to understand the natural environment

Children's Books
Compost Stew by
 Mary McKenna Siddals
*Garbage Helps Our Garden Grow:
 A Compost Story* by
 Linda Glaser
How Does Your Garden Grow? by
 National Geographic Society

Materials
bucket
compost (see activity on page 88)
garden string
old jug or watering can
old plates or lids, big enough to cover the top of a bucket
small burlap sack
smocks or T-shirts
string
water

Preparation
• This is a fun but slightly messy project. Children need to wear the appropriate clothes or have on smocks or old T-shirts.

What to Do
1. Place seven or eight handfuls of compost inside the sack. Tie the top shut with a piece of string.
2. Fill your bucket about three-quarters of the way with water.
3. Tie the string ends to the bucket handle, then drop the compost-filled sack into the water.
4. Rest an old plate or lid on top of the bucket so your stewing "tea" is covered.
5. Leave for five to seven days.
6. Scoop out the tea with an old jug or small watering can, and use it to water your plants.
7. Repeat the process once every two to three weeks, if desired.

Tip: The aim of compost tea is to provide a nutritional treat for plants and gardens, helping them to thrive. If you only have indoor or potted plants, they can still benefit, although it's probably best to water them with this mixture outdoors, before returning them to their usual positions.

Kirsty Neale, Orpington, Kent, UK

Planting a Theme Garden

Learning Objectives: To develop the skills of planning, decision-making, and patience; to develop small and large motor skills; to learn gardening vocabulary

Children's Books
Jack's Garden by Henry Cole
Mrs. Spitzer's Garden by
    Edith Pattou
Our Generous Garden by
    Anne Nagro
Whose Garden Is It? by
    Mary Ann Hoberman

Materials
planting area or pots
seeds and plants for the selected theme
shovels or trowels
water and watering cans or a hose

Preparation
- Secure permission, if needed, for planting space for the theme garden, or plan to plant in dirt-filled pots.
- Ask parents to donate plants or seeds appropriate to the theme you have chosen.

What to Do
1. There are many theme gardens that children can easily grow from seeds or plants: a butterfly garden, a garden of edible flowers, a kitchen garden, and a vegetable garden are some examples. Let children select the theme for the garden, either by guided discussion or by vote.
2. Help the children plant seeds according to package directions and water the seeds.
3. Let the children aid in setting in plant or herb seedlings that do not grow well from seed.
4. Be sure to take the children out every few days to check on the progress of their garden. Water and weed when necessary.
5. When the seeds sprout and bloom or the plants are ready to harvest, guide the children to enjoy the butterflies, the scent and color of the flowers, or the taste of the herbs or fresh vegetables from their theme garden.

Tip: Once the theme garden is growing, invite parents, grandparents, and caregivers to enjoy the garden with the children. If the theme garden contains food, help the children prepare salads or vegetable dips for their guests on their special day.

Kay Flowers, Summerfield, OH

Soil Samples

Learning Objectives: To develop an awareness of all five senses; to increase oral language skills

Materials
magnifying glasses
pencils or craft sticks
plastic spoons
white paper plates
zipper-seal plastic sandwich bags

Children's Books
Dirt: The Scoop on Soil by
   Natalie Rosinsky
A Handful of Dirt by
   Raymond Bial
Soil Basics by Mari C. Schuh

Preparation
- Find a place near your school yard where you can take a small sampling of soil. Visit the location of the soil in advance of this activity to make sure the soil has been recently turned over and aerated.

What to Do
1. Read books about soil with the children. Talk about what soil is and how it provides nutrients to plants.
2. Gather the children outdoors near the bed of soil, and give each child a paper plate and a spoon. Encourage them to feel, smell, and observe the soil. Talk about their observations.
3. Ask the children to place several spoonfulls of soil onto their paper plates and then find a space to work with a partner.
4. Encourage the children to use a pencil or craft stick to break apart any chunks of soil and to move the soil around on the plates for better observation. Have children describe what they see, feel, and smell as they explore the soil.
5. Give the children magnifying glasses so they can look for smaller insects or details in the soil.
6. Provide the children with zipper-seal plastic bags. Suggest that the children fold their plates in half, and then use them to "funnel" the soil into the bags.
7. Encourage children to take the soil home to show and tell their family what they learned about soil.

Mary Murray, Mazomanie, WI

Chapter 9: Bubbles, Air, and Sky

What do kites, bubbles, pinwheels, feathers, clouds, flags, and streamers have in common? By playing with them or watching them, we can observe and learn about the way air moves. Use the activities in this chapter to start learning, then branch out and let the children play with a wide variety of materials. They will enjoy experiencing the wind that comes before a storm, the gentle breezes of spring, and the fun of creating their own wind by blowing through a straw or running with scarves streaming behind them. You may be caught up in their delight!

Bubbles, Bubbles Everywhere

Learning Objectives: To learn about the properties of bubbles; to find new ways to make bubbles

Materials

bubble wands in a variety of sizes

bubble solution (purchased or use your favorite bubble recipe)

clean water

different items to use as bubble blowers, such as tubes, toy kitchen tools, and so on

large tub or water table that can be moved outdoors

towels

What to Do

1. Set up a bubble station by pouring lots of solution into a water table or large tub.
2. Put out a variety of bubble wands, and let the children experiment with blowing bubbles.
3. After the children have had some experience blowing bubbles, let them select items to try to use as bubble blowers. They might choose kitchen toys, their fingers, or any waterproof item. Let them experiment to see what works and what does not work.
4. Save all the bubble makers that work, and make a classroom list of the names of the items that work. Send the list home with the children, along with a recipe for making bubble solution.

Tip: Two hands, with finger and thumbs connected together and dipped in bubble solution, make great bubbles.

Children's Books

Bubble Bubble by Mercer Mayer

Bubble Trouble by Margaret Mahy

Pop! A Book About Bubbles by Kimberly Brubaker Bradley

Ann Scalley, Orleans, MA

Bubble Fun

Learning Objectives: To improve eye-hand coordination; balance; and large motor skills such as bending, jumping, and hopping

Materials
bubble mixture
bubble wands

What to Do

1. Purchase bubble mixture or make the bubble recipe on this page.
2. Have the children form a circle. Demonstrate how to burst a bubble by touching it with your finger. Move around the circle, blowing bubbles and letting the children burst them.
3. Ask someone to pop the bubbles by clapping both hands together. Move around the circle, blowing bubbles and letting each child clap to pop them.
4. Demonstrate stomping bubbles and have the children do the same.
5. Have the children jump high into the air to bat the bubbles with their hands. Blow the bubbles well above their heads.
6. Instruct the children to raise one foot, and then hop on a bubble when it lands.
7. Have the children pretend that their feet are stuck to the ground. Continue blowing bubbles and tell them to lean, bend, and stretch without falling over to pop the bubbles.
8. Tell the children to burst the bubbles using only their knees, then their elbows, and then their wrists. Ask them come up with other ideas.

Tip: It is fun to blow bubbles on a windy day and let the children watch how the wind carries the bubbles away in one direction.

Bubble Fun Recipe
Mix the following together:
1 tablespoon liquid detergent
½ teaspoon sugar
4 ounces water

Cindy Bosse, Crystal Springs, MS

Bubble Play

Learning Objectives: To develop small and large motor skills; to distinguish between *larger* and *smaller*

Materials
bubble solution
extra towels
large and small bubble wands
plastic bowls or tubs
waterproof tablecloth (optional)

Preparation
- Cover the work space with a tablecloth, if desired.
- Pour the bubble solution into the different containers.
- Add the bubble wands to the bowls and tubs.

What to Do
1. Talk with the children about what the words *large* and *small* mean.
2. Invite the children to play with the bubble wands and to try making large and small bubbles.
3. Ask the children about the bubbles they are creating. How do they make smaller bubbles? How do they make larger bubbles? How do they make a lot of bubbles? How do they make just one?
4. Refill the tubs and bowls when solutions are getting low.
5. Help the children rinse and dry their hands when they are finished.

Children's Books
How to Make Monstrous, Huge, Unbelievably Big Bubbles by David Stein
Pop! A Book About Bubbles by Kimberly Brubaker Bradley

Tina R. Durham-Woehler, Lebanon, TN

Cloud Shapes

Learning Objective: To use imagination and observation skills

Materials
large blankets or several towels

What to Do
This simple activity is relaxing and fun on a beautiful day.

1. On a nice day with lots of clouds, take the children outside and have them spread the blankets or towels on the ground.
2. Encourage the children to lie on the ground with you, look up into the air, at the sky, and observe the clouds. What shapes do they see? Are any clouds moving or changing?
3. Help the children use words that describe the shapes, sizes, locations, and colors of the clouds.

Children's Books
The Cloud Book by Tomie dePaola
Hi, Clouds by Carol Greene
It Looked Like Spilt Milk by Charles G. Shaw
Little Cloud by Eric Carle
Weather Words and What They Mean by Gail Gibbons

Sandy L. Scott, Meridian, ID

3+

Color Bubble Catch

Learning Objective: To develop large motor skills

Materials
bubble blowers
construction paper
liquid soap
plastic containers
tempera paint, different colors
water

Children's Books
The Big Orange Splot by
    Daniel Manus Pinkwater
It Looked Like Spilt Milk by
    Charles G. Shaw

What to Do
No worries about spills when you do this outside!

1. Pour liquid soap, water, and a small amount of tempera paint into the plastic containers. Cover and shake well to mix.
2. Demonstrate how to blow bubbles using a bubble blower, and encourage the children to practice blowing bubbles.
3. Show the children how to catch the bubbles on a piece of paper. The bubbles will burst and leave an impression on the paper.
4. Let some children be blowers and some be catchers, then change roles so everyone can make a bubble-catch picture.

Tip: Make different-shaped bubble blowers by bending straws or coat hangers. Does this change the shape of the bubbles?

Tip: Make different-shaped bubble blowers by bending straws or coat hangers. Does this change the shape of the bubbles?

Barbara Saul, Eureka, CA

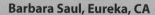

Let's Air–Periment!

Learning Objectives: To experiment with air and its ability to move objects; to develop critical thinking skills

Materials

plain paper (optional)

straws (nonbendable)

heavy things that can't be blown with air puffed from a straw: blocks, dolls, and so on

light things that can be blown with a puff of air from the straw, such as craft feathers, marbles, paper wads, very small toys, small balls, leaves, and so on

Children's Books

Air by Victoria Parker

Air by Henry Pluckrose

Air Is All Around You by Franklyn M. Branley

Air: Outside, Inside, and All Around by Darlene Stille

What to Do

1. Read a book or two about air to the children.
2. Discuss air and wind. What do the children know about air? What experience do they have with strong winds?
3. Talk about the meanings of the words *light* and *heavy*.
4. Take children outside on a windy day and let them feel the power of the wind.
5. When the wind dies down, place one of the objects on the ground or a sidewalk. Show the children how to puff air through the straw to try moving the object.
6. Let the children experiment with what they can move and what they cannot move. If one child puffing air does not move an object, can two or more children puffing air move an object?

Tip: Have plenty of straws! If you want to expand this activity, fold pieces of paper concertina-style into simple fans. Use the fans to create wind. Is this wind stronger than the wind you create by blowing through a straw?

Donna Alice Patton, Hillsboro, OH

BUBBLES, AIR, AND SKY

Chart the Rain

Learning Objectives: To develop an understanding of measurement; to introduce simple addition

Materials
calendar
rain gauge, or a plastic jar with straight sides, and a ruler

What to Do
Relate this activity to your explorations of clouds. (See pages 101 and 102.)

1. Set the rain gauge outside on an open, level spot.
2. Every time it rains, the rain gauge will collect water.
3. After the rain, read the rain gauge with the children, or use the ruler to measure the amount of water in the container. Then empty the rain gauge so it is ready for the next rainfall.
4. Chart the daily amount of rain on a calendar, and discuss it with the children.

Tip: Cut a piece of ribbon the length that you measured for each day's rainfall during one week or, for a challenge, one month. Calculate the total rainfall for the week or month by lining the ribbons up end to end and measuring the total length.

Barb Lindsay, Mason City, IA

Cloud Collecting

Learning Objectives: To learn about weather and clouds; to develop small motor skills; to practice descriptive language

Materials

blue construction paper
white crayons

What to Do

This activity can be repeated many times in different weather conditions.
Some days you will see only one kind of cloud, other days there will be several kinds to observe. Is there ever a day "without a cloud in the sky"?

1. Read a book about clouds, look at cloud pictures, introduce the names of different kinds of clouds, and discuss different types of clouds with the children.
2. Ask the children to look up at the sky. What do they see in the sky today: Low, flat stratus clouds? Tall, puffy cumulus clouds? High, wispy cirrus clouds? Encourage the children to describe the clouds in their own words.
3. Explain that clouds are made of water vapor (tiny droplets of water) like the steam in the bathroom after someone takes a shower. As the water vapor rises higher in the atmosphere where the air is colder, the droplets cool, cluster together, and fall as rain or snow.
4. Hand out the paper and crayons. Encourage each child to draw one or more of the clouds they see.
5. Back in the classroom, hang their cloud pictures on a wall. If possible, hang high clouds near the top of the wall and low clouds near the bottom.

Children's Books

The Cloud Book by
 Tomie dePaola
Clouds by Marion Dane Bauer
Clouds by Anne F. Rockwell
Shapes in the Sky by
 Josepha Sherman

BUBBLES, AIR, AND SKY

**Sue Bradford Edwards,
Florissant, MO**

5+

BUBBLES, AIR, AND SKY

I Spy a Cloud in the Sky

Learning Objectives: To identify the characteristics of cirrus, stratus, and cumulus clouds; to develop creative expression and vocabulary

Materials

child-safe scissors

cloud photos

construction paper: blue, white, and gray

cotton balls

crayons, chalk, markers, colored pencils, and plain pencils

glue

white paper of various weights and textures, including tissue paper

Children's Books

The Cloud Book by Tomie dePaola
Cloud Dance by Thomas Locker
Fluffy, Flat, and Wet: A Book About Clouds by Dana Meachen Rau
It Looked Like Spilt Milk by Charles Shaw
Little Cloud by Eric Carle
Shapes in the Sky: A Book About Clouds by Josepha Sherman

Preparation

• Find pictures of different cloud types you can show the children. The Internet is a good resource for these pictures. (See below.)

What to Do

This activity expands on the creativity of the Cloud Collecting activity found on page 101.

1. Ask the children to look up at the clouds. What kinds of clouds can they see?

2. As children are looking, find a cloud that looks like a familiar object. Say, "I spy a cloud in the sky, and it looks like a _____. Who can find it?" Let several volunteers try to guess which cloud you spy. Let them take turns leading the I Spy game.

3. Introduce cloud types. Show a picture of cirrus clouds and describe their characteristics: high, thin, wispy clouds made of ice crystals. Pull apart a cotton ball until the strands are thin and wispy. Demonstrate gluing this "cloud" onto the gray paper, and label it *cirrus*.

4. Next, introduce stratus clouds: low, grayish clouds made of water droplets. Show the picture and create a stratus cloud by "teasing out" a cotton ball until it is long and fairly flat. Glue this "cloud" onto the white paper, and try darkening it a bit with pencil or chalk. Label this cloud as *stratus*.

5. Finish by introducing cumulus clouds: white, puffy clouds with a flat base. Show a picture and create a cumulus cloud by gluing a number of cotton balls close together onto the blue paper. Label this cloud as *cumulus*.

6. Now offer all the materials to the children and let them create cloud picture collages of their own. They may wish to recreate your pictures of different cloud types; they may wish to create clouds that look like bunny rabbits or baseball mitts; they may wish to create a thunderstorm. Let their imaginations blossom!

Tip: Use the following websites for visuals and additional information:
http://www.weatherwizkids.com/weather-clouds.htm
http://eo.ucar.edu/webweather/cloud3.html
http://www.kidskonnect.com/subject-index/15-science/67-clouds.html

Kathryn Hake, Lebanon, OR

Chapter 10: Light and Shadow

Discover the fascinating world of light and shadow. Bring the children outside on a sunny day and try these activities. Try your ideas, and ask the children for their ideas. After you have played and investigated light and shadow outdoors, ask some of the same questions when you are indoors. What is the same? What is different?

3+

Shadow Rhymes

Learning Objective: To develop phonemic awareness, large motor skills, and attention span

Materials
sunny day

Preparation
- Locate a sunny area outdoors where you and the children can gather.

What to Do

1. Chant or sing these simple rhymes outdoors. Model the motions for the children and encourage them to join you in saying the words and doing the motions.

My Shadow
© 2011 MaryAnn F. Kohl
I have a shadow, and so do you.
Can you see your shadow?
I can, too.
Jumping, hopping, (act out this part)
Waving, flopping.
Dancing, stopping.
I have a shadow, and so do you.
Can you see your shadow?
I can, too.

Sing a Song for Shadows
© 2011 MaryAnn F. Kohl
(To the tune of "Sing a Song of Sixpence")
Sing a song for shadows,
Shadows big and small.
See my funny shadow
Dancing on the wall.
Shadows are like friends
Who play on sunny days.
How I wish my shadow friend
Would never go away.

2. Can you make your shadow extra tall? Can you make your shadow disappear inside your friend's shadow? There is a lot to observe.

MaryAnn F. Kohl, Bellingham, WA

Shadow Walk

Learning Objectives: To improve observation skills; to enhance small and large motor development; to develop oral language skills

Materials

sidewalk chalk
sunny day

What to Do

1. On a sunny day, take the children outside to see how many interesting shadows they can find.
2. As you take your walk, look for shadows from all sorts of objects, for example, the shadow cast by a chain-link fence, a tree, playground equipment, and so on.
3. Talk about how your shadow moves as your body moves. Have the children stand with their backs to the sun and strike various poses.
4. Ask the children to work with a classmate to draw each other's shadows with sidewalk chalk on the pavement. Can they make the shadows tell a story?

Children's Books
Moonbear's Shadow by Frank Asch
My Shadow by Robert Louis Stevenson and Glenna Lang
Shadow by Suzy Lee
Shadows and Reflections by Tana Hoban
Whose Shadow Is This? by Claire Berge

Jackie Wright, Enid, OK

4+

Shadow Tag

Learning Objective: To develop observation skills and large motor control

Materials

large outdoor area

sunny day

Children's Books

Gregory's Shadow by Don Freeman

Moonbear's Shadow by Frank Asch

My Shadow by Robert Louis Stevenson and Glenna Lang

What to Do

This familiar, traditional game is a lot of fun!

1. Talk with the children about shadows.
2. Ask the children to look at one another's shadows. Can they tell whose shadow belongs to whom?
3. Invite the children to play tag. Pick a child to be "it," but, instead of touching another child, the person who is "it" will try to step upon someone's shadow.
4. If a child's shadow is stepped upon, then she becomes "it."

Tip: You can make this into a game of Shadow Freeze Tag by having the child who is "it" shout "Freeze!" when she steps on someone's shadow. Everyone must "freeze" like statues until the new "it" shouts "Unfreeze!" and the game of tag resumes.

Sandy L. Scott, Meridian, ID

Shadow Time

Learning Objectives: To learn about shadows; to practice observation skills

Materials
sidewalk chalk
sunny day

What to Do

1. Help the children find the shadows cast by benches and playground equipment.
2. Help them trace these shadows with sidewalk chalk directly onto the blacktop or sidewalk.
3. Ask the children how they expect the shadows will look later in the day. Will they stay the same? Will they grow? Will they shrink? Will they move? What if the sun goes behind a cloud?
4. Go back inside, and read a book about shadows.
5. About two hours later, go outside. Are the shadows still in the outlines? Help the children to see how the shadows have changed.
6. Help the children trace the new shadows. How are they different? How are they the same?

Tip: If you have the same group for a full day, begin this activity first thing in the morning and then revisit the shadows two or three times throughout the day.

Children's Books
Moonbear's Shadow by Frank Asch
Shadows and Reflections by Tana Hoban
What Makes a Shadow by Clyde Robert Bulla
Whose Shadow Is This? by Claire Berge

**Sue Bradford Edwards,
Florissant, MO**

Tracking Changing Shadows

LIGHT AND SHADOW

Learning Objective: To practice observation skills and cooperation

Materials
shadows
sidewalk chalk
sunny day

Preparation
- This activity will be completed over time during the day; plan your schedule accordingly.
- Locate a large area on a sidewalk or the blacktop that receives full sun throughout the day.

What to Do
1. Point out their shadows to the children.
2. Ask the children if they know what makes a shadow. Explain that when we stand in the way of the sun's rays, we cast a shadow. As the sun moves throughout the day, our shadows move, too.
3. Ask one child to stand feet together on the sidewalk. (If necessary, reposition the child so her shadow is totally on the sidewalk.) Trace around the child's shoes with chalk. Draw a line at the top of the child's shadow. Write the child's name and the time on the line and her name on the shoe tracing.
4. Invite other children to have their feet outlined, to help draw around feet, and to mark lines at the top of shadows. Label each shoe tracing with the child's name and each line with both the name and the time.
5. After an hour, come back to the shadows. Ask the children to stand on their feet outlines. Ask, "What has happened to your shadow?" (The children may explain that the shadow shortened, got smaller, lengthened, grew, or changed direction.) Mark a new line and label it, if desired.
6. Continue this procedure throughout the day. Shadows will shorten during the morning hours, nearly disappear at high noon, and lengthen in the afternoon.

Tip: See "Sundials" on page 112 to explore a similar idea.

Rob Sanders, Brandon, FL

Shadow Play

Learning Objective: To practice observation skills, critical thinking, cooperation, and large motor control

Materials
butcher paper
crayons
scissors
sunny day

Children's Books
Shadows and Reflections by Tana Hoban
Whose Shadow Is This? by Claire Berge

Preparation
- Cut sheets of butcher paper as long as the tallest child, one for each child.

What to Do
1. On a sunny day, start a conversation with the children about shadows. Do we see shadows outdoors every day? Shadows are created when an object blocks light.
2. Go outside and look around for shadows. Suddenly you will see them everywhere! Does a shadow look exactly like the thing it is a shadow of? How are they the same? How are they different?
3. Place a piece of the butcher paper on the ground and ask one child to stand at the edge of it so her shadow is clear on the paper. Trace the shadow with a crayon.
4. Discuss with the children how the shadow is like the child and how it is different from the child. Is it the same size? Are some features unclear?
5. Now ask the same child to lie down on the same sheet of butcher paper. Trace the outline of her body in another color of crayon.
6. Assist pairs of children as they trace each other and their shadows. How are the shadow outlines different from the body outlines?

Debbie Vilardi, Commack, NY

LIGHT AND SHADOW

Sundials

5+

Learning Objective: To learn how the position of the sun in the sky changes during the day

Materials
camera
pictures of sundials
smaller colored sticks
yardstick or long dowel

Preparation
- Select a spot that will receive full sun all day and won't be disturbed.

What to Do
This is a good activity to do after you have done some of the other shadow explorations in this book. Then the children will bring some basic understandings to this more abstract concept.

1. First thing on a sunny morning, talk about shadows. Review what the children already know.
2. Go outside to your chosen spot. Tell the children that as the sun moves across the sky during the day, shadows cast by the sun also move. We can use these shadows to mark the passage of time.
3. Poke the yardstick into the ground, and lay a smaller stick along the shadow. Take a photo, and record the time. Explain that you will check on the shadow throughout the day.
4. With the children, return to the same spot every hour, marking the new position and length of the shadow with a small stick, taking a photo, and recording the time.
5. Each time, discuss how much the shadow has moved. Has it changed in any other way?
6. Toward the end of the day, introduce the word *sundial,* and talk about how people learned to tell time before we invented clocks and watches. Show the children photos of sundials.
7. Ask the children if they have any ideas about why the shadow moves. Accept all responses!

Debbie Vilardi, Commack, NY

Chapter 11: Animals and Insects

There is a natural affinity between children and other living things. Outdoors is the perfect setting for this relationship to grow and blossom. Use the following activities to guide and encourage children to share the earth with our fellow creatures respectfully and lovingly.

Wormy Exploration

Learning Objectives: To develop observation skills; to practice measurement and counting

Materials

dirt (Note: Do not use commercial potting soil. It can contain chemicals and additives that are potentially harmful to both children and worms.)

earthworms (these can be purchased at a bait shop or fishing supply store or, with permission, can be dug up from a garden area)

plastic tub

rulers

small buckets or plastic cups

Children's Books

Diary of a Worm by Doreen Cronin

It Could Still Be a Worm by Allan Fowler

Preparation

• Place the worms into a tub filled with dirt.

What to Do

1. Read a book about worms. Talk about what worms do for our soil.
2. Give the children small buckets or plastic cups. Remind the children that they need to be gentle with the worms. Let the children take turns reaching into the dirt to find a worm to study.
3. Encourage the children to measure their worms. How would they describe their worms?
4. Try counting all the worms. How many are in the tub?
5. When the children are finished examining their worms, return the creatures to the tub, and find a nice garden in which the worms can live.

Sarah Stonebraker, Seattle, WA

Animal Charades

Learning Objectives: To learn about animals; to follow directions

Materials

pictures of a variety of animals, both wild and domestic (be sure to include animals that might be familiar to the children already)

What to Do

This is a simple activity that can be done indoors or out. If you "Take It Outside!" it will have more meaning, and the children can be more active.

1. Read a book about animals and the sounds they make.
2. Look at some photos of different animals, and ask the children if they know how each animal moves and what sounds it makes.
3. Divide the children into two groups. Whisper an animal name to one group while the other waits. The first group will then move around like that animal, making its distinctive sounds. The second group will try to guess the name of the animal.
4. Repeat, giving the second group a chance to act out an animal.

Children's Books

Animals Aboard! by Andrew Fusek Peters
Animals Speak by Lila Prap
Moo, Baa, La La La! by Sandra Boynton
Sounds All Around by Wendy Pfeffer

Susan Oldham Hill, Lakeland, FL

Birds Fly

Learning Objectives: To improve large motor skills; to practice color identification; to observe and learn about birds

Materials

bird identification book or photographs of various birds in select colors

scissors

six colors of crepe paper streamers: red, orange, yellow, black, brown, blue

Children's Books

About Birds: A Guide for Children by Cathryn Sill

Birds, Nests and Eggs by Mel Boring

National Geographic Backyard Guide to the Birds of North America by Jonathan Alderfer

Preparation

- Cut two or more 12" lengths of streamer for each child to hold; use the select colors listed above.
- Look through the bird books ahead of time so you are familiar with some of the birds in your area.

Note: If you do not have streamers in the select colors, simply use strips of scrap fabric or art paper, or cut wing shapes from colored cardstock or craft foam.

What to Do

1. Look at the bird books with the children. Talk about the various types of birds, taking note of the color of each select bird. Point out any birds that the children might see in your outdoor play area or in their neighborhoods. Talk about how birds move.
2. Go outside, gather the children into a circle, and give each child two streamers of the same color, to be their "wings."
3. Ask the children to spread out a bit to give themselves room.
4. Call out a bird name and a color; ask the children with that color of "wings" to fly around the outside of the circle, then return to their places. Encourage the children to flap their wings and move like birds.
5. Continue until all of the birds have had a chance to stretch their wings.

Mary Murray, Mazomanie, WI

Butterfly, Butterfly, Where Are You?

Learning Objective: To practice recognizing geometric shapes

Materials
clothespins
markers
paper cutouts of butterflies of different sizes
tape or glue

Preparation
- Make paper cutouts of butterflies.
- Draw shapes onto the wings: circles, triangles, squares, and so on. (Draw only one type of shape per butterfly.)
- Glue or tape the clothespins onto the butterflies.
- Clip the shape butterflies onto bushes, fences, and play equipment.

Children's Books
Are You a Butterfly? by Judy Allen
Caterpillars and Butterflies by Stephanie Turnbull
How to Hide a Butterfly by Ruth Heller
Now I Know: Look . . . a Butterfly by David Cutts
Where Butterflies Grow by Joanne Ryder

What to Do
1. Read a book about butterflies. Ask the children what details they notice: wings, colors, antennae, and so on. Many butterflies have easily recognizable shapes in the patterns on their wings.
2. Go outside and gather the children for a butterfly hunt. Show them one of the butterflies you made with a specific shape on its wings—for example, a triangle. Review the different shapes with the children, if necessary.
3. Ask them to go find the matching butterfly and return it to you. Continue until all the butterflies are found.
4. Look at the butterflies together, and talk about the different shapes on each.

Tip: The children may be interested in comparing the paper butterflies with the butterfly pictures. This could be a rich exploration.

Carol Hupp, Farmersville, IL

4+

Butterfly Flight

Learning Objectives: To develop large large-muscle coordination; to practice following directions

Materials
none

What to Do

1. Teach the children "Butterfly." Say the words of the poem rhythmically to establish the beat for flapping wings.

Butterfly by Rob Sanders

Tiny little butterfly
Unfold your wings.
You can do it, just you try.
Tiny little butterfly
Unfold your wings.
Now you're ready, soar and fly!

Medium little butterfly
Flap your wings.
You can do it, just you try.

Medium little butterfly
Flap your wings.
Now you're ready, soar and fly!

Great big butterfly
Spread your wings.
You can do it, just you try.
Great big butterfly
Spread your wings.
Now you're ready, soar and fly!

2. During the "Tiny little butterfly" stanza, encourage the children to move just their hands from the wrist to form flapping wings.
3. For "Medium little butterfly," encourage them to put their fists to their chests and flap their elbows to form wings.
4. During the "Great big butterfly" stanza, encourage them to extend their arms and flap.
5. Lead the children on a nature walk, perhaps to visit flowers, guiding them to follow in a line as they repeat the poem and flap their wings.
6. Let the children fly free like butterflies around the outdoor play area.

Tip: You can change the words of the poem to act out birds, crawling insects, climbing animals, and so on.

Rob Sanders, Brandon, FL

Finding Home

Learning Objective: To learn about animals and animal homes

Materials

pictures of animals that live in the homes: bird, ant, wasp, rabbit, spider, hermit crab, turtle, and so on (laminated if possible)

pictures of various animal homes: bird's nest, anthill, wasps' nest, rabbit burrow, spiderweb, shell, pond, and so on (laminated if possible)

Tip: The Internet is a good source of photos of animals and their homes.

Children's Books
Animals at Home by Craig Brown
Animals at Home by David Lock
Whose House Is This? by Elizabeth Gregoire

What to Do

1. Read a book about animals and their homes.
2. Discuss the types of homes various animals have. What animal homes have the children seen? You can enrich the exploration by pointing out animal homes in storybooks you have read.
3. Show the children pictures of a variety of animal homes. Can they guess what animal lives in each home?
4. Let the children use the pictures of animals and animal homes outdoors as inspiration to create animal homes in their play.

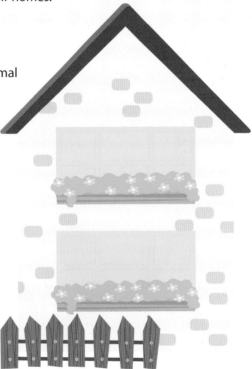

Sue Bradford Edwards, Florissant, MO

How Large Is a Whale?

Learning Objective: To learn about measurement and about relative sizes

Materials

100-foot tape measure (purchase this at a building-supply store)
chalk or stones to use as markers
children's books about whales
pictures of whales

Children's Books

Face to Face with Whales by Flip and Linda Nicklin
Is a Blue Whale the Biggest Thing There Is? by Robert E. Wells
The Snail and the Whale by Julia Donaldson
The Whales' Song by Dylan Sheldon

What to Do

1. Read about whales. You will learn that there are many species of whales, ranging in size from the blue whale, which can be up to 100 feet in length (This is approximately the length of three school buses!), to the pygmy sperm whale, which averages 11 feet long.
2. If you have a large enough outdoor area, help the children measure the length of a blue whale and mark it on the blacktop with chalk, or on the grass with stones or other markers.
3. Have the children lie down, head to foot, along the length of the whale. How many children would it take to be as long as a blue whale?

Sandy L. Scott, Meridian, ID

Move Like an Ant

Learning Objectives: To learn about ants; to practice following instructions

Materials
basket or bowl
large ball of yarn
simple snack food, a piece for each child (graham crackers, for example)

Children's Books
Ant Cities by Arthur Dorros
Are You an Ant? by Judy Allen
Inside an Ant Colony by
 Allan Fowler

Preparation
- Shortly before snack time, put the bowl of snacks on an outdoor picnic table and cover it if necessary.
- Unroll the ball of yarn from the classroom door to the picnic table. Create an interesting, round-about route

What to Do
1. Read a book about ants and talk about ants with the children. Almost everyone will have had some experience with ants. Encourage them to talk about it.
2. After they have shared what they know, explain that ants look like they are following each other because they are all actually following a scent trail. When one ant finds food, it leaves a trail for other ants to follow.
3. Tell the children that today they are going to be ants and follow a scent trail to their snack.
4. Help the children wash their hands and line them up at the classroom door.
5. In single file, they must follow the leader along the yarn "scent trail" to the snack table.

**Sue Bradford Edwards,
Florissant, MO**

Seashell Sorting

Learning Objectives: To learn about shells; to practice sorting by color and shape; to practice ordering by size

Materials
blankets or beach towels
sand play area
shallow pans, such as cake pans or pie tins
variety of empty shells: clam, scallop, mussel, and so on
water

Children's Books
Seashells by the Seashore by
Marianne Berkes
Smithsonian Handbooks: Shells
by S. Peter Dance
What Lives in a Shell? by
Kathleen Weidner Zoehfeld

Tip: Some children may want to bring seashells from home to share and talk about.

Preparation
- Collect a variety of empty shells. You can buy them at a craft store if necessary.

What to Do
1. Read a book about shells and seashore life. Depending on the ages and interests of the children, you may want to explain that seashells are the hard outer parts of animals called *mollusks*. A mollusk has a soft body that needs the protection of a hard shell. Mollusks make a chalky juice that hardens into a shell. As the animal grows, it makes its shell larger. When mollusks die, their empty shells wash up on the beach for you to find.
2. Spread out your collection of shells and talk about them: their sizes, their shapes, their colors. Do any of the children have experiences at a beach they would like to share?
3. Go outside to the sand play area, bringing the shells, the beach towels or blankets, and the shallow pans with you.
4. Fill the pans with water and nestle them into the sand play area. Put the shells in the pans filled with water.
5. The children can build sand castles, hide and find shells, sort the shells by color or shape, and order the shells by size. There are many creative learning possibilities.

Marianne Berkes, Hobe Sound, FL

Those Scampering Squirrels

Learning Objectives: To develop observation skills; to describe and demonstrate what was observed

Children's Books
The Busy Little Squirrel by Nancy Tafuri
Nuts to You by Lois Ehlert
The Tale of Squirrel Nutkin by Beatrix Potter

Materials

children's books about squirrels
outdoor area with trees and squirrels

Preparation

• Find an outdoor area where you can bring the children to play and see squirrels.

What to Do

You can find squirrels somewhere in almost any neighborhood: city or country. Take advantage of this to introduce the children to animals living in their habitats.

1. Read some books about squirrels with the children. Talk about squirrels. Have they seen them? where? What do they know about them already? Leave the books available for the children to look at again after they have been outside.
2. Take the children outside to the playground or a park that has trees. Sit quietly on the ground for a few minutes and watch for squirrels.
3. Notice what the squirrels are doing: Are they running? climbing? eating acorns? balancing on the telephone wire? Squirrels build nests of dry leaves on the limbs of trees. Can you spot any of these nests?
4. Once you have identified some "squirrely" behaviors, ask two or three children at a time to act like squirrels. Be sure that everyone who wants a turn has one.
5. Introduce this simple chant:

> Squirrels can climb,
> Squirrels can run.
> Scamper, scamper, scamper,
> Squirrels have fun.

Gryphon House Staff

5+

Actively Animal

Learning Objective: To learn about measurement and comparison

Materials
painter's tape or other colored tape
pen
tape measure

Children's Books
Actual Size by Steve Jenkins
Kangaroos by Diane Swanson
Nature's Best Jumpers by Frankie Stout

Preparation
- On an outside wall, mark off and label the height of a turkey (48 inches), a wolf (26 inches), and a tiger (36 inches). Add animals that are common to your area.
- On the ground, mark the starting point for the long jump. Then mark and label these distances: kangaroo (29 feet), bullfrog (6 feet), and grasshopper (2 feet). Add animals that are common to your area.

What to Do
1. Explain that the children are going to test themselves to see how they measure up in the animal kingdom. Are they as tall as a turkey? Can they jump as far as a kangaroo?
2. Have them line up along a wall. Add their heights to the wall with tape, and label each piece of tape with the children's names. Who is the tallest? the shortest? Is there a cluster of children approximately the same height?
3. Ask the children to compare their heights to those of the turkey, wolf, and tiger. Are they taller or shorter?
4. Lead the class to the starting point for the long jump. From here, each child gets to jump once. Measure each jump, and mark it with tape; label the tapes. Whose jump is the longest? the shortest? Is there a cluster?
5. Ask the children to compare their jumps with those of the kangaroo, bullfrog, and grasshopper. Are they longer? shorter?

**Sue Bradford Edwards,
Florissant, MO**

Chapter 12: Dramatic Play

Children's dramatic play and the outdoors go together like peaches and cream. Most of the time, all you need to do is to bring some props outside and let the children invent their own dramatic play scenarios. At other times, you may want to focus and direct their play, or you will want an activity to reinforce a particular concept you are teaching. At those times, turn to this chapter for creative ideas created by experienced teachers.

Dino Steps Game

Learning Objectives: To develop large motor skills; to practice following directions

Materials
none

What to Do

1. Read a book about dinosaurs and other prehistoric animals. Talk with the children about how different dinosaurs and prehistoric animals may have moved. For example, a tyrannosaurus took big, wide steps; a pterodactyl may have flapped its wings as it hopped; an apatosaurus took heavy, stomping steps; a saber-toothed tiger walked quietly and growled.

2. This is a variation of the game Mother, May I? Help the children form a row on one end of the play area.

3. Call out each child's name and the name of a prehistoric animal. Encourage the children to move like that animal. For example, *Jamie, you may take three tyrannosaurus steps forward. Marcos, you may take five pterodactyl steps. Amy, you may take two saber-toothed tiger steps.*

4. Proceed until all the children have reached your position in the play area.

Related Children's Books
Dinosaurs! by Gail Gibbons
Let's Look at Dinosaurs by Frances Barry

Susan Arentson Sharkey, Fletcher Hills, CA

Going Camping

Learning Objective: To develop large motor skills, vocabulary, and imagination

Materials

camping gear, such as a small tent, sleeping bags, backpacks, small cooler, plastic utensils and tableware, hiking boots, child-sized fishing poles (no fishing hooks or fishing line), and so on

What to Do

1. Talk with the children about camping. Read a book about camping, and ask the children what kinds of items they would need on a pretend camping trip. Some children may have been camping with their families. Encourage them to share their knowledge and experiences.
2. Have the children help you take the camping materials outside. Choose a campsite, and help them set up camp.
3. Encourage the children to decide where they will sleep, how they will cook their meals, and how they will store their food.

Tip: These props can lead to other kinds of dramatic play. Think of pioneers and Antarctic explorers, for example.

Children's Books

Going on a Bear Hunt by Michael Rosen

Just Me and My Dad by Mercer Mayer

S Is for S'mores by Helen Foster James

Toasting Marshmallows: Camping Poems by Kristine O'Connell George

When We Go Camping by Margriet Ruurs

Tina R. Durham-Woehler, Lebanon, TN

Canoeing

4+

Learning Objective: To develop large motor skills

Materials

fallen log or a picnic bench or a low balance beam

What to Do

1. Talk about canoes and canoeing. (This activity ties in well with "Going Camping" on page 127 and "From Here to There" on page 130.)
2. If you have an outdoor area with a fallen log, take the children to that area. If not, find a picnic bench or a low balance beam so the children can sit astride.
3. Have four children sit astride the bench or log and pretend to hold paddles. Show them how to make fists with both hands, putting their fists together and making a paddling motion, first on one side, then on the other.
4. Explain to the children that they are on a river and they need to paddle to move the canoe along the river.
5. Act out the paddling motions while singing "Row, Row, Row Your Boat," or the following song.
    "A-Canoeing We Will Go" (to the tune of "A-Hunting We Will Go")
    A-canoeing we will go
    A-canoeing we will go
    We'll dip our paddles in the water
    And down the river we'll go.

Children's Books

Antler, Bear, Canoe: A Northwoods Alphabet Year by Betsy Bowen
Canoe Days by Gary Paulsen
One-Dog Canoe by Mary Casanova
Three Days on a River in a Red Canoe by Vera B. Williams

Dianne Leschak-Halverson, Chisholm, MN

Dining al Fresco

Learning Objective: To develop social studies concepts and vocabulary

Materials

cardboard or poster board (optional)
crayons (optional)
notepads
paper
pencils
plastic plates, cups, and utensils
serving trays
variety of kitchen implements and utensils, such as pots, pans, large spoons, spatulas, muffin tins, tablecloths, and so on.

Children's Books

Dim Sum for Everyone! by Grace Lin
Froggy Eats Out by Jonathan London
Going to a Restaurant by Melinda Beth Radabaugh
Minnie's Diner: A Multiplying Menu by Dayle Ann Dodds

Tip: Ask families for donations of old pots, pans, and other unbreakable kitchen utensils.

What to Do

1. Read a book about a restaurant. If appropriate, talk with the children about their experiences in restaurants. Who did they go with? Who works in a restaurant? Allow the children to share their experiences and knowledge.
2. Encourage the children to set up an outdoor restaurant. Help them set up eating and cooking areas. What foods will they serve? (Sand, grass, leaves, and rocks make excellent pretend foods. Just remind the children not to put these items into their mouths!)
3. Provide cooking utensils, trays, notepads and pencils for taking orders, eating utensils, and tablecloths, if desired.
4. Consider helping the children to make a sign for their restaurant and menus for the patrons to "read."
5. Let the children decide who will be cooks, who will be waiters, and who will be the restaurant patrons.

Ann Scalley, Orleans, MA

DRAMATIC PLAY

From Here to There

Learning Objectives: To develop listening skills, large muscle coordination, and social studies knowledge

What to Do

1. Call attention to different modes of transportation in the storybooks you read over the course of a few days. Use the suggested books as additional resources.

2. With this experience as background, talk about the different ways people travel today in the United States of America, and how we traveled in the past. Today we can walk, ride a bicycle, drive a car, or ride in a bus, a train, or an airplane. What was it like for your grandparents? What is it like in other countries?

3. Now, *"Take It Outside!"* and explain that you are going to do some pretend traveling. Name an environment and encourage the children to pretend to travel in that environment. In many cases, there will be several options. For example: If you pretend the play area is a big desert you need to cross, you could drive if there is a road; you could ride on a camel if there is no road; you could fly over it in an airplane if you are in a hurry.

4. Suggest many different scenarios and let the children use their imaginations, their knowledge, and their whole bodies to demonstrate how they would get around.

Tip: This play can evolve in many directions. Use your own creativity, and let the children use theirs.

Children's Books

Airplane! Soaring! Diving! Turning! by Patricia Hubbell
Getting There by Marla Stewart Konrad
How We Get Around by Rebecca Rissman
I Like Riding by Bobbie Kalman
Let's Go: The Story of Getting from Here to There by Lizann Flatt
On the Go by Ann Morris
Trains: Steaming! Pulling! Huffing! by Patricia Hubbell
We All Go Traveling By by Sheena Roberts

Sue Bradford Edwards, Florissant, MO

130   LET'S TAKE IT OUTSIDE

My Favorite Rock

Learning Objectives: To develop observation skills; to learn vocabulary to describe and compare rocks; to learn about geologists

Materials
buckets
paper towels
sand
sandbox
shovels
variety of rocks
water

Children's Books
Everybody Needs a Rock by Byrd Baylor
If You Find a Rock by Peggy Christian
The Magic School Bus Inside the Earth by Joanna Cole and Bruce Degen
Stone Soup by Marcia Brown

Preparation
• Hide rocks of various colors, shapes, and sizes in the sandbox.

What to Do
1. Read a book about rocks. Discuss what a geologist does.
2. Pretend to be geologists and go on a rock-hunting expedition. Have the children dig in the sand and collect as many of the hidden rocks as they can find.
3. Gather the rocks together and have the children wash them off with water.
4. Ask the children to sort the rocks by color, size, or shape.
5. Encourage the children to talk about the rocks and to compare them. Does anyone have a favorite?
6. After the children have compared and examined the rocks, they may choose to stack and arrange the rocks in patterns or build with them.

Tip: The children might enjoy having a field guide to rocks and minerals available to look at, such as *Smithsonian Handbooks: Rocks and Minerals* by Chris Pellant.

Marcia Beckett, Madison, WI

DRAMATIC PLAY

Dino Dig

Learning Objective: To learn what a paleontologist is and how fossils are found

Materials

hats
large spoons and small shovels
paintbrushes
shells, twigs, leaves, and other natural objects
sieve or framed screen
toy dinosaurs

Children's Books

The Best Book of Fossils, Rocks and Minerals by Chris Pellant
Bones Rock! by Peter Larson and Kristin Donnan
Dinosaur Bones by Bob Barner
Fossil by Claire Ewart
The Fossil Girl: Mary Anning's Dinosaur Discovery by Catherine Brighton

Preparation

- Bury the dinosaurs, and the shells, twigs, leaves, and other natural items in the sandbox.

What to Do

1. Ask the children what they know about dinosaurs.
2. Read a book about fossils and how they are found. Explain that although dinosaurs disappeared long ago, we know about them because scientists called paleontologists have found their bones, called fossils.
3. When you go outside, encourage the children to pretend to be paleontologists. (They can wear hats, such as sun visors.) Tell the children that they can search for pretend dinosaurs, shells, and leaf fossils buried in the sandbox.
4. Introduce the sieve or screen and demonstrate how to sift sand. When a child spies or touches an object, tell her to stop sifting or digging. Show her how to use a paintbrush carefully to unearth the object.
5. Let the children use shovels and large spoons to lift the fossils out of the sand and then show their discoveries to the class.

Tip: Here are some websites with games, activity papers, and information about dinosaurs:

http://www.kidsdinos.com/

http://www.search4dinosaurs.com/

http://dsc.discovery.com/dinosaurs/

http://resources.kaboose.com/games/dino.html

http://funschool.kaboose.com/time-warp/dinosaurs/

http://www.primarygames.com/science/dinosaurs/dinosaurs.htm

Christine Kohler, Ballinger, TX

Pass the Torch

Learning Objectives: To practice large motor and cooperation skills; to learn about the Olympics

Children's Books
G Is for Gold Medal: An Olympics Alphabet by Brad Herzog
The Pickle-Chiffon Pie Olympics by Jolly Roger Bradfield
Tacky and the Winter Games by Helen Lester

Materials

empty paper-towel roll
gold spray paint (adult only)
paper streamer
red, yellow, and orange tissue papers
tape

Preparation

- Use an empty paper-towel roll to make a torch by decorating it with gold spray paint and attaching tissue-paper flames to the top.
- Design an interesting path for the torch runners. Place a paper-streamer finish line at the end of the path.
- Create a place to put the torch at the end of the course so it can be "kept burning" as long as the Olympic games continue.
- If desired, place flags of various countries along the course or around the play area.

What to Do

1. Read a book about the Olympics. Explain the significance of the Olympic torch and that it is passed from person to person. The torch is passed from the country where the games were held to the country the games are taking place. The torch burns the entire two weeks of the games. It is an honor to carry the torch.
2. Tell the children that they will each have a chance to carry an Olympic torch and pass it along.
3. Let the children arrange themselves all along the course you have laid out. Hand the torch to the first child, and let each child have a chance to run a piece of the course and pass the torch to the next person in line.
4. As the children pass the torch, encourage them to cheer on their classmates and friends until the torch finally crosses the finish line.

Tip: You can create many large motor activities and playground Olympic games: the children can "swim," hop, sideways walk, backward walk, skip, gallop, crabwalk, bearwalk, fly like a bird, jump, and many more.

Tina R. Durham-Woehler, Lebanon, TN

Chapter 13: Large Motor Skills

The outdoors offers young children a joy-filled setting for the development of their large motor skills, coordination, and muscle strength. Give the children as much freedom as possible to run, jump, skip, and fly to their hearts' content. If we cultivate and support children's natural love of active outdoor play, we will be enhancing their lifelong health and well-being. What better legacy can we offer them?

Amazing Maze

Learning Objectives: To develop motor control; to follow directions; to practice teamwork

Materials

3' stakes

obstacles such as boxes, balls, lawn chairs, blankets (to drape over the chairs) large toys, or buckets

rope

Preparation

- Set up an obstacle course using a variety of items the children can safely crawl under and over, walk around, or climb through.
- Establish the edges by using rope tied to stakes to create a boundary line.

What to Do

1. Show the children the way through the obstacle course. They must crawl through, go under, hop over, and so on!
2. Encourage the children to explore and navigate the obstacle course. Help them as necessary.

Jean Potter, Greensburg, PA

Hoop Play

Learning Objective: To enhance balance, coordination, large motor skills, imaginative play, and listening skills

Materials
balls or beanbags
construction cones
rope
several large plastic hoops
string or Velcro strips

Preparation
- Set up a variety of stations for the children to practice their motor skills.

What to Do
1. Hang a hoop on a tree branch or from a piece of playground equipment. Have the children toss balls or beanbags through the hoop.
2. Tie several hoops together with string or Velcro strips and place them flat on the ground. Let the children practice hopping in the hoops like in hopscotch. (Note: Younger children can hop as many times as needed inside each hoop.)
3. Encourage the children to roll hoops up and down a hill or incline. Or stand a distance from a fence and roll the hoops into the fence. How far can you roll the hoop before it falls over?
4. Using construction cones, let the children toss the hoops like horseshoes.
5. The children will make up their own additional games.

Bev Schumacher, Racine, WI

Leaves in the Parachute

Learning Objectives: To practice following directions; to develop large muscle coordination

Materials

large parachute or bedsheet

real fall leaves (if available) or paper cutouts

Tip: Substitute leaves with any abundant natural material in your area. For example, you can do this activity with small pinecones or flower petals.

Children's Books

I Am a Leaf by Jean Marzollo

Leaves! Leaves! Leaves! by Nancy Elizabeth Wallace

Red Leaf, Yellow Leaf by Lois Ehlert

We're Going on a Leaf Hunt by Steve Metzger

What to Do

1. Lay the parachute or sheet out flat on the ground. Help the children space themselves around the edge of the parachute.

2. Walk around the children with a supply of leaves, and let each child throw some of the leaves onto the parachute.

3. Ask the children to reach down, grab the edge of the parachute with both hands, and while holding onto the parachute, stand up straight. Explain that they are going to make the leaves fly up into the air. When you count to three, have all the children raise their arms up quickly to lift the parachute above their heads. Have them repeat this as long as they are interested.

Tip: Vary the game by lifting slowly and then fast. Try shaking the parachute really fast. Try having the children lift the parachute as you call a child to run under the parachute. Put some leaves under the parachute and have a child run under, grab a leaf, and run out.

Sandra Ryan, Buffalo, NY

Flying Fun

Learning Objectives: To practice using directional words; to follow directions

Materials

What to Do

1. Teach the children this song, sung to the tune of "I've Been Working on the Railroad":

   I Am Flying in a Circle by Susan Oldham Hill

   I am flying in a circle, (The children move around the perimeter of a circle, arms extended.)
   Soaring through the air.
   Now, I'll turn and change directions. (The children turn, face opposite direction, and move again.)
   I see soft clouds everywhere!
   Watch me as I fly down lower; (The children squat closer to the ground.)
   And now I soar up high; (The children stand again.)
   I dip my right wing toward the ground and (The children dip their right hand down.)
   My left wing toward the sky. (They lift left "wing" up.)

2. Explain to the children that they will stand in a circle and "fly" around like birds.
3. Ask the children to extend their arms like wings and "fly" like birds. Begin singing the song with them, asking them to move in one direction.
4. Encourage the children to follow the directions given with the song.

Children's Books
Circles of Hope by
   Karen Lynn Williams
So Many Circles, So Many Squares
   by Tana Hoban

Susan Oldham Hill, Lakeland, FL

LARGE MOTOR SKILLS

Loopity Hoop

Learning Objectives: To develop motor skills and listening skills; to understand directions; to recognize colors

Materials

plastic hoops in a variety of colors

Preparation

• Place different colored hoops around an open outdoor space.

What to Do

1. Let the children warm up in an open area. Provide the children with ideas for moving around: walk, hop, skip, run, walk sideways, walk backward, and so on.
2. Demonstrate ways to walk or run around the hoops without touching them; let the children explore ways to move in and among the hoops.
3. After the children are comfortable moving around and among the hoops, add instructions such as, "Stand in groups of two inside the red hoops" or "Three people go into each green hoop."
4. Provide another kind of direction, such as, "Put your hand into a hoop," or "Put your foot into a yellow hoop."

Jean Potter, Greensburg, PA

Red Light, Green Light, Yellow Light

Learning Objectives: To practice large motor skills and impulse control; to practice listening skills

Materials

What to Do

1. Talk with the children about traffic lights and signs. Talk with the children about why we need traffic lights (to help avoid accidents and maintain the flow of traffic in an orderly manner).

2. Ask the children what the different colors of the lights mean: red for *stop,* green for *go,* and yellow for *slow down and prepare to stop.* Let the children offer their ideas first; they may know what the colors mean already.

3. Introduce the game of Red Light, Green Light, Yellow Light by demonstrating stop on red, go on green, and slow down on yellow. Make your "slow down" movement like a slow motion movie. The children will love it!

4. Have the children line up a few yards away from you, and call out the light colors as the children proceed toward you using the appropriate movements. The "slow down" movement may be the hardest for the children to accomplish, as it requires a good deal of balance and coordination.

5. The first child to reach you by using the correct movements gets to take your place and call out red, green, or yellow light directions.

Tip: Some children have difficulty with impulse control and will benefit from kind words that reward them for appropriate behavior: "Look how carefully Bobby is moving when it's a yellow light." "Wow, Anita, you really stopped quickly!"

Children's Books

City Signs by Zoran Milich
Green Says Go by Ed Emberley
I Read Signs by Tana Hoban
Outdoor Safety by Nancy Loewen
Road Safety by Sue Barraclough

Kay Flowers, Summerfield, OH

Simon Says

Learning Objectives: To practice listening carefully and following directions; to learn about animals; to develop large motor skills

Materials

What to Do

1. Ask the children to show you several different animal movements. Suggest a few, such as waddling like a duck or leaping like a frog.

2. Tell the children that you are going to play a listening game. You will call out the name of an animal, and they will make a noise or move like that animal. Some examples:

- Waddle like a duck.
- Leap like a frog.
- Crow like a rooster.
- Slither like a snake.
- Hop like a rabbit.
- Bark like a dog.
- Stretch your neck like a giraffe.

- Flap your wings like a bird.
- Gallop like a horse.
- Snort like a pig.
- Trumpet like an elephant.
- Wave your arm like an elephant's trunk.
- Roar like a lion.
- Snap like a crocodile.

3. If you like, when the children have become proficient at moving like different animals, explain that you are going to add a rule. They have to wait for you to say, "Simon says," before they can move like the animal you call out. Let them practice a few times, then try the new game.

Jackie Wright, Enid, OK

Walk and Count

Learning Objectives: To develop listening skills and coordination; to practice following directions

Materials

What to Do

1. Take the children for a walk. You can walk in the community around the school, on the playground, or even inside the school on a rainy day.
2. As you walk, say silly things for the children to do, such as:

    Take two big steps and three little steps.

    Take three little steps, hop one time, and take three big steps.

    Take one little step, turn around two times.

    Hop four times, turn around one time.

    Take three big steps forward and two big steps backward.

3. Count aloud as the children perform each action.
4. Let the children take turns telling the group silly things to do as you walk.

**Virginia Jean Herrod,
Columbia, SC**

LARGE MOTOR SKILLS

Roll It UP!

Learning Objective: To practice taking turns, working together, and using arm muscles to roll a ball up an inclined plane

Materials
small plastic sand pail or bucket
small soft balls

Preparation
- Place the bucket and balls near the slide.

What to Do
1. Gather the children and tell them that they are going to play a game called Roll It UP! Have one child volunteer to go to the top of the slide and hold the bucket so the opening is facing the slide. Make sure the bucket is touching the slide.
2. Give another child a ball. Tell him that he will roll the ball UP the slide to the bucket and see if he can get it in.
3. Help the children catch the ball as it comes back down.
4. Let the children take turns trying to get the ball into the bucket and take turns being the bucket-holder.

Tip: This game requires a slide on a playscape that has a platform behind the slide. If you have more than one slide, you can have more than one game going at a time, so more children can join in the fun.

Shelley Hoster, Norcross, GA

Index

LET'S TAKE IT OUTSIDE